Lives of the Great
Poisoners

plays by Caryl Churchill

CHURCHILL PLAYS: ONE
   Owners, Vinegar Tom, Traps, Light Shining in Buckinghamshire,
   Cloud Nine

CHURCHILL PLAYS: TWO
   Softcops, Top Girls, Fen, Serious Money

SERIOUS MONEY

SOFTCOPS and FEN

TOP GIRLS
   (also published in the Methuen Student Edition with commentary and
   notes)

ICE CREAM

MAD FOREST

Lives of the Great Poisoners

A PRODUCTION DOSSIER

Text by Caryl Churchill
Musical score by Orlando Gough
Movement notes by Ian Spink

Methuen Drama

First published in Great Britain in 1993
by Methuen Drama
an imprint of Reed Consumer Books Ltd
Michelin House, 81 Fulham Road, London SW3 6RB
and Auckland, Melbourne, Singapore and Toronto
and distributed in the United States of America
by HEB Inc, 361 Hanover Street, Portsmouth,
New Hampshire NH 03801 3959

A CIP catalogue record for this book
is available from the British Library
ISBN 0 413 67070 8

Typeset in 11/12 pt Plantin Linotron
by Wilmaset Limited, Birkenhead, Wirral
Printed in Great Britain
by Clays Ltd, St Ives plc

CAUTION
This play is fully protected by copyright. All rights reserved
and all enquiries concerning the rights for professional or
amateur stage productions should be made to Casarotto Ramsay Ltd,
60 Wardour Street, London W1V 3HP. No performance may be given
unless a licence has been obtained. All enquiries concerning the
musical score should be made to Orlando Gough, c/o Methuen Drama.
All enquiries concerning the movement notes should be made to
Ian Spink, c/o Harriet Cruikshank, 97 Old South Lambeth Road, London SW8 1XU.

Contents

Illustrations

1. Laboratory: The massage dance. (Photo: Robin Morris)
2. Floor raised to wall position (early model).
3. Death of Creusa: Periodic table.
4. Music Hall Song: 'She poisoned him, he poisoned her. They both took an antidote.' (Photo: Rosy Sanders)
5. Detail from *Interior* (*The Rape*), 1868–1869 oil on canvas, 32″ × 45″ by Edgar Degas, French (1834–1917). Philadelphia Museum of Art: the Henry P McIlhenny Collection in Memory of Frances P McIlhenny.
6. Cora's Death: 'Be quiet, someone will hear you.' (Photo: Robin Morris)
7. On the Ship: Cabalistic woman.
8. On the Ship: 'Large pieces of human remains.' The Sailor attempts to get the hatbox from the sleeping Crippen. (Photo: Rosy Sanders)
9. On the Ship: Crippen, Ethel and the Dolphin dance. 'If you'd listened to me they wouldn't have got away.' (Photo: Rosy Sanders)
10. Corinth: Medea: 'I want her dead.' (Photo: Rosy Sanders)
11. Medea's Triumph: 'Yes, I can bring the dead to life. But not for you.' (Photo: Rosy Sanders)
12. Detail from *Extreme Unction* by Nicholas Poussin (Picture Gallery) (c) English Life Publications Ltd. By kind permission of the Duke of Rutland, The Belvoir Estate.
13. On the Ship: Medea: The hand.
14. Laboratory: 'You do nothing. The days pass. You grow old. You die.' (Photo: Rosy Sanders)
15. Detail from *The Cheat with the Ace of Clubs*, about 1630, oil on canvas, 97.8 × 156.2cm. by Georges de la Tour, French (1593–1652). Kimbell Art Museum, Fort Worth, Texas.
16. Hoca: (Photo: Rosy Sanders)
17. The Casket: 'What do you know?' Mme de Brinvilliers is given the water torture. (Photo: Rosy Sanders)

Laboratory: The massage dance. Sally Owen.
(Photo: Robin Morris)

Introduction *by Caryl Churchill*

In 1979 I saw *The Seven Deadly Sins* at the Coliseum, with Julie Covington singing one Anna and Siobhan Davis dancing the other, and thought of working with three performers, one of whom would speak, one dance and one sing. But it was ten years before I worked on that kind of piece.

Meanwhile, I saw Trisha Brown talking while she danced, the Pina Bausch shows at Sadlers Wells in 1982 and work by Second Stride, and gradually got nearer to working with dancers. Les Waters and I asked Ian Spink and Siobhan Davis to work with us on the project that became *Fen*, but neither of them was free. There was a string quartet and a choreographed riot in Howard Davies' production of *Softcops* at the RSC. *Midday Sun* (1984) was a collaboration arranged by John Ashford with performance devisers Geraldine Pilgrim and Pete Brooks; Sally Owen, a Second Stride performer, was the choreographer. In 1986 Les Waters and I approached Spink again and he worked with us and writer David Lan on *A Mouthful of Birds* for Joint Stock. The piece was made during twelve weeks, the writing mainly done in the middle four. Some of the performers were mainly dancers and some mainly actors, but everyone took part in the large movement pieces and everyone had spoken parts, though there were places where dancers danced and the actors had more to say. *Fugue* (Channel 4, 1988) was a film with a final dance piece, using movements that had happened in the story.

The big difference with *Lives of the Great Poisoners* was singing. Orlando Gough, Spink and I started meeting every few weeks and decided quite soon to have singers who sang, dancers who danced and actors who spoke, rather than everyone doing everything. This would mean scenes between, say, a character who spoke and one who sang or one who sang and one who danced. Orlando decided he wanted the singing to be *a capella*, which had two big effects. One was that he needed four singers; we felt there should be the same number of dancers (it was after all a Second Stride show) and since cost meant we could only have nine performers this left only one place for an actor, so we decided to bend our rule and make one of the performers both sing and speak. The other effect was that the words had on the whole to be written first. This, combined with our decision that – because the rehearsal period would be short – the words and music should be written before it started, meant they were more or less fixed before the movement was made. This doesn't mean that the text constantly dominates what happens. 'Death of Creusa and Creon – dance. They are sung to death by Medea and Poisons,' left everything to Orlando and Spink. Sometimes the text is conversational, although Midgley moves in and out of song and Crippen and Cora speak and sing to each other. Sometimes it's more like verse ('If I put my hand in fire.') Sometimes it's bits of documentary ('Brinvillier's confession.') Sometimes it's just a few words which are used for a far longer piece of music ('Don't kill yourself.')

I think it was Orlando who started us on poison and we played around for some time with the idea of a toxic waste ship of fools unable to put in to any port. That faded but poison stories stayed. Midgley, an American inventor discovered by Spink, turned out to be a way of turning three stories into one. So did spotting love triangles – Cora murdered by Crippen could come back for her revenge as Medea, and the story fell into place. There would be Crippen/Jason/Sainte-Croix (actor), Cora/Medea/Brinvilliers (singer) and Ethel/Creusa/Mme Sainte-Croix (dancer), and their friend Midgley. After that the details of the story were fairly quick to work out. There was soon a scenario we all agreed on and I went off to write the words, sending scenes to Orlando as I went on. At the beginning of rehearsal some characters had large parts down on paper while others still had their parts to be made. Similarly this book gives more weight to the sung and spoken characters because description and photographs can only give a glimpse of what was going on physically throughout the piece.

Some background information: Crippen's name as a poisoner is well known, though the details of his story may not be. Lequeux was a prolific writer of mystery novels; Crippen apparently wrote to him with ideas for plots involving perfect murders. His reading is made up of quotations from 'An Eye for an Eye'. Everything Crippen says to Ethel is taken from his letters to her. Medea's story is too well known to need telling here. Less well known is that she also used her knowledge of potions to restore youth, as she did for Jason's father Aeson. Brinvilliers was a notorious poisoner in seventeenth-century France. She learned about poison from her lover Sainte-Croix, who learned from Exili, an international political poisoner. Many of Mme de Sevigny's lines are taken from her letters. 'Brinvilliers' Confession' is based on her written confession. Thomas Midgley was an American industrial chemist in the early part of this century. He put the lead in petrol and CFCs in fridges, two inventions that seemed a good idea at the time but were inadvertently poisonous. An idea he never put into practice was that surplus corn production in America could be restricted by increasing the ozone in the earth's atmosphere. Our Midgley has no resemblance to the real Midgley, apart from these inventions. In the Brinvilliers section he is based on her children's tutor, Briancourt.

Introduction *by Orlando Gough*

I have always looked enviously at cultures in which music and dance have a natural alliance; in particular in which musicians and dancers have a natural alliance. In our culture, an alliance between musicians and dancers is jeopardised by the existence of the composer and choreographer, who act as a kind of medium between the idea and the performers. The composer and the choreographer may work very closely together – but what about the musicians and the dancers? Dancers often rehearse to taped music and are introduced to a live version of the music late in the rehearsal period. An anxious time of adjustment follows. The dancers think, understandably: 'Why can't these idiots play it as it is on the tape? Why is the tempo unreliable? Why can't we hear the piano entry properly? . . .' In the worst case, the musicians and the dancers never meet. The musicians play in a different space (the pit) from the dancers and there is an atmosphere of mild mutual distrust and a terrible sense of hierarchy: the musicians are there simply to service the dance.

I have struggled, particularly in my previous collaborations with Ian Spink and Antony McDonald, to find solutions to this problem, while realising that my own contribution as a composer is part of the problem. I am interested to see musicians and dancers working together on stage so that the audience may be aware of the physicality of the music-making as well as the physicality of the dancing. Often the musicians have been involved in the stage action with the dancers, but I have always felt that instrumentalists in this situation are hampered not only by their lack of acting experience but also by their instruments.

So it seemed a good idea to make a piece in which none of the performers needed any props. (A violin, a *prop*? Well, in the context of stage action, yes.) So the musicians would all be singers. Since we had decided to make a narrative piece, all the musicians would be involved in playing character roles, so that all the emotional intensity, all the drama of the music would come from the stage (unlike a Wagner opera, for instance, where the orchestra always seems to have the best tunes). The incidental advantage of *a cappella* music is that it is much easier to hear the words, the disadvantage that it is very difficult for the singers to keep in tune over long

xi

periods. (We ended up with the musical director giving discreet, occasional help on a synthesiser; after a few performances the singers could probably have done without.)

Because it is a dramatic piece where the singers are playing characters who are seldom in agreement and most usually in tension with each other, it was seldom possible to write close harmony – a pity – so most of the music is counterpoint of some kind. In order to create a good vocal texture, I always included as many singers as possible in each scene, often giving a singer an accompanying vocal line derived from a tiny fragment of text, and sometimes, when no text was needed, a scat vocal line – where there is no text in the score, the notes should be sung to suitable invented syllables. Even so, the texture is very thin. Musically, this is perhaps a disadvantage. The advantage is that it allows a natural transition between spoken and sung text and passages of spoken dialogue for the actors can become part of a vocal number without being overwhelmed (for example, the 'Hoca' scene). The fact that the score contains very few dynamic markings does not by any means imply that I intend the singing to be flat and inexpressive, rather that the dynamics should be dictated by dramatic considerations – partly by the meaning and emphasis of the words and partly by their balance. In a group number, variations of dynamics can be used to move the focus of attention from one character to another.

So, from one point of view, the piece is like a play in which some of the dialogue happens to be sung; but I was also trying to keep in mind that it is at the same time a dance piece, and to write music that would inspire movement. In particular, the lengthy 'Death of Creusa and Creon' is intended specifically as a dance number. The music tells the story of their deaths; but there is scarcely any text – the singers sing syllables that I chose for their sound rather than for their meaning. The story-telling takes on a different form here – the story is still being told, but there is a greater level of abstraction due to the dancing and lack of text. The technique is like that of a nineteenth-century narrative ballet, except that the musicians are on stage and involved in the action. When the singers sing these meaningless syllables, they are in the strange position of being half in, half out of character. Fortunately singers do not seem to mind this ambiguity as much as actors.

The roles of all four singers are at least as demanding as that of a principal singer in an opera; for, as well as the intrinsic difficulty of each part, the lack of instrumental support leaves them with an unusually heavy mutual responsibility – in fact, they need to have the cohesiveness of a string quartet, sympathetic to the nuances of each other's performances, while playing very diverse characters. *And* they have to act well enough to exist on stage with an actor. *And* move well enough not to look lumpish on stage with dancers . . . I wrote the piece with jazzy, bluesy voices in mind, but in fact none of the singers in the first production had voices of this kind. There were two opera singers, one who specialised in contemporary music and an actor with a wonderful natural voice. While the score is simple by contemporary music standards, it is complex (and very long!) by most pop and jazz music standards. It was a great advantage to have singers who were technically secure and could read music; in fact, we reluctantly had to replace a superb jazz singer with extensive experience of *a cappella* music, as he couldn't learn his part – a problem aggravated by not being able to read music.

The success of our eventual casting made me realise the advantage of having four singers with varying backgrounds. The music has a strange, ambiguous texture which is very appropriate to the narrative.

We allowed the singers two weeks' preliminary rehearsal on the music alone and wished we'd allowed more; ideally, they needed to be a confident, cohesive *a cappella* group with the music in their heads, before starting to rehearse with the rest of the cast.

So what about the alliance of dance and music? Well, we managed to make a piece in which there was no hierarchy of musicians and dancers and in which they were able to rehearse productively for a long period; but the problem of the composer and choreographer as middle-men remained. It turned out to be just another experiment in linking dance and music, but from my point of view a very instructive and worthwhile one.

Introduction *by Ian Spink*

Since its formation in 1982 Second Stride has developed a habit of attempting a marriage of mixed theatre forms (text, music, performance and dance) with the result that its productions are often difficult to define. A critic once wrote 'Is it dance, opera or theatre? Who cares, it's great.' The work to which he was referring was *Heaven Ablaze in his Breast* (1989) a collaboration which involved composer Judith Weir, designer Antony McDonald and myself. Based on a story by E T A Hoffmann, the piece was performed jointly by Vocem Electric Voice Theatre and a group of Second Stride dancers. All the performers shared singing, dancing and spoken text and *Heaven Ablaze* probably fitted more into the category of music theatre.

Lives of the Great Poisoners was already in the planning stages well before *Heaven Ablaze* hit the stage. It marked the return of composer Orlando Gough to the company after three years' absence and included a writer, Caryl Churchill, for the first time. Caryl and I had worked together before under different circumstances: *A Mouthful of Birds* (Joint Stock, 1986) and *Fugue* (Channel 4/ Dancelines, 1988). Both of these productions required dancers and actors to share disciplines. However for *Poisoners* we decided that the performers would rarely if ever stray from their individual disciplines. Thus the singers would sing their parts in the manner of opera, the actors would act their parts and the dancers would dance their parts, neither speaking nor singing.

Orlando took the brave step of planning an *a cappella* score, that is, sung and spoken text without instrumental accompaniment. Music uttered from the stage would energise the narrative along with a series of 'choreographed' scenes and characterisations. The music and the text were initially the backbone of this work and a constant reference point during rehearsals.

The choreography for the four dancers began after the score and text had been developed. Improvisations with the performers led to movements which were later developed separately into dances which were then fitted into the written scenes.

The large mixed-form scenes ('Whist', 'Music Hall Song', 'Death of Creusa' and 'Hoca') began as separate layers of text, music and choreography and were woven together so as to allow each element its own integrity. As one who has moved away from pure dance, my main concern was that there should never be a flagging in the narrative line nor indeed in the layers of the texture. For me this meant a subtler kind of dance, one that could appear out of the action as if from nowhere.

During the script development period we spent much time matching the multitude of potential characters from our three stories with the particular skills of our chosen performers. There were aspects of the original characters in our source material which led us to decide what kind of performer should play each part and also provide a central trio of singer/dancer/actor.

The dancer characters were divided thus: Ethel, strong but shy, was reputed to have had 'frog feet' in her childhood. She assisted Crippen in his quack treatments for patients with hearing problems. We decided that she should communicate with an invented sign language. This sign language later informed the radio/semaphore communication used to trap Crippen as he tried to escape to America. Her reincarnation, Creusa, dies as a result of wearing a poisoned dress, suggestive of much anguished physical movement and a counterpoint to the death of Cora in the Crippen section. As the wife of Sainte-Croix she is unable to say or do anything about his infidelity with Mme de Brinvilliers, except for a final mute confrontation at the end of the piece when she refuses to give up his casket of incriminating love letters and poisons.

Marie Lloyd, a respected music-hall performer, was well known for her innocent yet suggestive stage shows. She was a friend of Cora Crippen and helped in the apprehending of the murderer Crippen. We decided that her theme should be ribbons in her stage show and flags in the 'Ship' section. In the 'Medea' section she becomes one of the poisons who impregnate the dress and kill Creusa. Later, in the 'Brinvilliers' section, she becomes an energetic and not so innocent mistress of the Marquis de Brinvilliers.

One of Cora's lovers was Bruce Miller. Ex-prize fighter turned music-hall entertainer he once had a one-man band act. Among other talents, his body and deft, mimed juggling hold a fascination for her. In reality the flashy Bruce eventually left Cora and returned to his wife in America. We have him transforming into Captain Kendall whose delicate investigative work leads to Crippen's capture aboard the SS Montrose. Later Kendall becomes the victim of Medea's poison in the person of Creusa's father, Creon. He returns again as the sad, wavering figure of the Marquis de Brinvilliers, prematurely aged and deformed by years of slow poisoning by his wife.

Aeson, the crippled father of Jason, who is restored to youthful movement by Medea's magic potion in the first section, later returns as Mr Martinetti, a music-hall friend of Cora whose speciality is funny walks and silly faces. He then becomes an energetic sailor on the SS Montrose helping Kendall uncover the escaping couple and communicating with semaphore to the shore. He returns in the Medea section to assist as a poisoner of Creusa. In the final section he becomes the mercurial and devilish La Chaussee, servant to Sainte-Croix and Mme de Brinvilliers.

Three of the dancers (and two of the singers), slip in and out of the roles of a Chorus of Poisons at various points during the piece (see breakdown of performers' roles).

Breakdown of Performers' Roles

M/Actor	M/Actor/Singer Baritone	F/Singer Soprano	F/Dancer
Jason		Medea	
Crippen	Midgley	Cora	Ethel
Jason	Midgley	Medea	Creusa
Sainte-Croix	Midgley	Mme de Brinvilliers	Mme Sainte-Croix

F/Dancer	F/Singer Mezzo-Soprano	M/Dancer	M/Singer Bass	M/Dancer
Poison	Poison	Aeson	Poison	Poison
Marie Lloyd	Mrs Smythson	Mr Martinetti/ Sailor	Lequeux/ Inspector Dew	Bruce Miller/ Capt. Kendall
Poison	Poison	Poison	Poison	Creon
Mme Dufay	Mme de Sevigne	La Chausee/ Desgrez's Asst.	Exili/ Desgrez	Marquis de Brinvilliers

The piece was made for four dancers, four singers (three singers, one actor/singer) and one actor.

Introduction *by Antony McDonald*

As Second Stride has emerged from the dance company it began life as in 1982, it has increasingly given great importance to the design of its productions – design, that is, not as decoration but as an essential part of the production. We have tried to push beyond the cliché of dance floor, painted backdrop and side-lighting. Each new production has tried to challenge the preconceived ideas of what a dance space might be, as we have aimed to challenge what a dance piece might be, blurring the line between choreography and design.

Often each piece has been a sort of reaction to or rejection of, in design terms, the piece that preceded it. So we moved from the monochrome cinematic coolness of *Further and Further into Night* in 1985 to the seemingly anarchic chaos of *Bosendorfer Waltzes* in 1986. In some ways the look of *Lives of the Great Poisoners* was a response to the complicated shifting scenery of the expressionist *Heaven Ablaze in his Breast*.

Although I was present at many initial meetings with Ian, Orlando and Caryl, it was not really possible to begin the design process until the whole libretto was finished and the music was written. I felt it was really important that the piece should feel like one narrative – one strange love affair, not three or four separate stories – and that the design should create very much its own world quite outside the Edwardian England of Crippen, the mythological Greece of Medea or the seventeenth-century France of Mme de Brinvilliers.

A further design challenge, too, was the fact that each section was made up of short scenes in a wide variety of locations that flowed one into another. The production was touring to several venues, so it was also important that the set had its own aesthetic dynamic that would look good and be commanding in differing spaces.

We were not interested in huge scene changes nor did we wish to offer an evening of furniture being dragged on and off stage. What emerged as the design was something quite abstract and sculptural that could change by means of hydraulics to create a series of spaces and planes. A permanent set made up of three units – three walls, one of which could also lower to become a floor at different angles. So we created interiors and exteriors, both open and private. Performers could appear above walls or around them and in the gaps or corridors between walls. They could be isolated in their own separate worlds and at the same time be overlooked by other performers. The set itself became, in turn, a drawing-room, a courtroom, a ship or two ships, a bed, a gaming table. There was never furniture to remove, so a scene with dialogue or singing could evolve immediately into dance and back again.

Projections were also thrown onto the light-coloured walls and floor of the set, not so much to define location but to give atmosphere. These were drawn from a wide number of sources – the paintings of Sickert, Degas and Matisse, various scientific diagrams, charts and symbols and anatomical drawings.

Again to increase the feeling of continuity and unity between the stories, the small number of props that we allowed ourselves reappeared in each section – so the hat-box that contained Cora Crippen's head became the vessel that held the poisoned wedding dress given to Creusa and then the casket of letters that contained the evidence that condemned Mme de Brinvilliers. All props had this multi-purpose.

The costumes were not related specifically to any period, although they made reference to several, but were designed again to create a world of their own. Corsets were used for both men and women, worn both on top of and underneath other garments. In a way in this production the corset served as the most obvious visual symbol of how we poison ourselves for personal vanity. Layers of clothing were removed as we moved through the different sections of the story. Thus the uptight pretensions of the lower middle-class Crippen world gave way to the exposed exhausted decadence of Sainte-Croix and Mme de Brinvilliers. As clothing was removed so make-up was added, as part of the self-poisoning process. Midgley stood apart from this scheme of things, dressed always in his forties suit.

Lives of the Great
Poisoners

Lives of the Great Poisoners was first performed at the Arnolfini, Bristol on 13 February 1991. The production was made possible with funds from the Arts Council of Great Britain and private donations. The cast was as follows:

Midgley, an industrial chemist — Michael O'Connor (actor/baritone)

Dr Crippen
Jason
Sainte-Croix, Mme de Brinvilliers' lover — Pearce Quigley (actor)

Cora, Crippen's wife
Medea
Mme de Brinvilliers — Angela Tunstall (soprano)

Ethel, Crippen's lover
Creusa, Jason's lover
Mme Sainte-Croix — Michele Smith (dancer)

Lequeux, novelist
Dew, police inspector
Exili, professional poisoner
Desgrez, Chief of Police — Józic Koc (baritone)

Aeson, Jason's father
Mr Martinetti
La Chausee, Sainte-Croix' servant
Degrez's Asst.
Sailor — Stephen Goff (dancer)

Mrs Smythson,
Mme de Sevigne — Jackie Horner (mezzo-soprano)

Marie Lloyd
Mme Dufay, Marquis de Brinvilliers' mistress — Sally Owen (dancer)

Bruce Miller, Cora's lover
Kendall, captain
Creon, Creusa's father, King of Corinth
Marquis de Brinvilliers — Michael Popper (dancer)

Chorus of Poisons — Stephen Goff, Jackie Horner Józic Koc, Sally Owen

Writer	Caryl Churchill
Composer	Orlando Gough
Musical Directors	Michael Haslam, John Lunn
Director	James MacDonald
Designer	Antony McDonald
Lighting Designer	Peter Mumford
Director/Choreographer	Ian Spink

Notes on Layout
Speech follows character name, sung passages are indented.
   A speech usually follows the one immediately before it but when one character starts speaking before the other has finished, the point of interruption is marked / .

Sections

Prologue:
Elixir of Life

Dr Crippen:
Evening at Hilldrop Crescent
Whist
Music Hall Song
Cora's Death
Suspicion
On the Ship

Medea:
Corinth
Death of Creusa and Creon
Lament for Creusa
Medea's Triumph

Mme de Brinvilliers:
Hospital
Laboratory
Hoca
Assignation
Morning After
Breakfast
Death of Sainte-Croix
The Casket
The Confession
Brinvilliers' Death

Elixir of Life

Medea *restores* **Aeson, Jason**'*s father, to youth.*

We hear wordless singing. **Medea**'s *assistants*
(**Chorus of Poisons**) *enter carrying objects which
include cup, knife, metal container (cauldron),
henbane, rubber toad. With one hand the dancers
gesture the preparations made for the ritual, digging
a pit, building a fire and collecting herbs.* **Medea**   I
*enters and takes the henbane and toad and throws
them in the pot. She goes into a spasm.* **Aeson,** *very
old and weak, is carried in by* **Jason** *and laid on the
floor.* **Medea** *takes the knife (see below), one of the
assistants places a cloth under* **Aeson**'s *head, and*
Medea *cuts his throat. His body is turned upside*   4
down to drain the blood. **Medea,** *using the cup,
takes magic potion from the cauldron and pours it
into the cut. He revives in a series of jerks. As the
others leave* **Aeson** *does a small youthful dance and*   6
bounds up the wall as it lowers into the next scene.

Medea   *Hurting you I heal you
Killing you I cure you
Secrets of death and new life
Poisons that heal
Fill your blood fill your breath
By my skill
I kill you and give you new life

Note: Figures at extreme right of dialogue provide a cross reference with score.
Sung passages are indented.

5

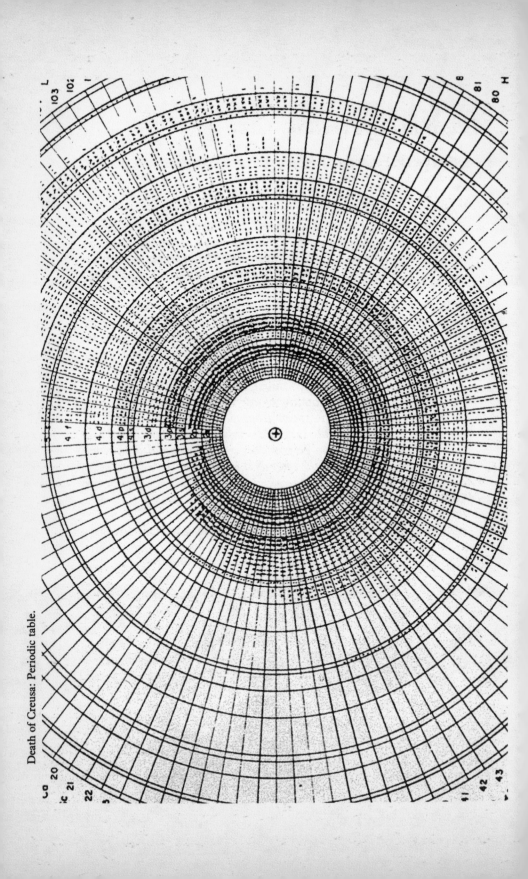

Death of Creusa: Periodic table.

Evening at Hilldrop Crescent

Crippen *and* **Midgley**. **Midgley** *is the Crippens' lodger.*

Midgley	Red was my first thought, the colour red. You want to guess how that came to me? You're a country boy. You ever seen the trailing arbutus that blooms under snow? That was magic to me. And what colour are those arbutus leaves? Red. Because the red absorbs the heat. So –
Crippen	I dont recall the leaves of the arbutus.
Midgley	Next time you go home to Michigan you take a look. So, red, if we could colour the fuel red, do you follow me?
Crippen	It would absorb heat –
Midgley	It would, it would vastly improve its combustion characteristics and, in a word, prevent knock.
Crippen	So you found a red dye –
Midgley	I found iodine. Homely old iodine your ma used to put on your cut knee. / And would you
Crippen	No, really? I remember –
Midgley	believe it? Iodine in the gas stops the knock.
Crippen	You'll make your fortune. / Mr Midgley, this is thrilling.
Midgley	A long way to go. Because it appears it's not after all the redness. The iodine, by odd chance, but not the redness. It appears to be a question of molecular structure. And iodine it turns out is not commercially viable. So now I'm in search of a new substance with the correct molecular structure.
Crippen	It's thrilling for me, Mr Midgley, to make the acquaintance of a scientist at the frontiers of knowledge. I know in my humble way how hard it is.
Midgley	Your own career has been devoted to science, / I believe.
Crippen	Humbly devoted to science and medicine. Always seeking new methods to lighten men's

7

	burdens. First with Munyon's Homeopathic
	Remedies. Then Drouet's Institute for the Deaf.
	Now the Yale Tooth Specialists. But of course I
	can hardly make a living. We are reduced to
	taking lodgers. In the case of a guest like yourself
	of course it's a pleasure and an honour.
Midgley	There's still time yet for both of us, Crippen.
Crippen	My latest little idea, I call it Sans Peine, the
	French gives it something, I'm about to take out
	a patent –
Midgley	There you are.

Lequeux *arrives.* **Crippen** *introduces him and*
Midgley.

Crippen	A great scientist and a great novelist meeting
	under my humble roof at Hilldrop Crescent. Mr
	Lequeux knows secrets thought dead with the
	Borgias which Mr Midgley and I as scientists
	would be fascinated to share. But first he has
	promised to read to us from his latest mystery.
Midgley	Great admirer. *Wiles of the Wicked, Whoso*
	Findeth a Wife, The Veiled Man.
Crippen	*The Day of Temptation, The Bond of Black, Secrets*
	of Monte Carlo.
Lequeux	*Eye for an Eye.*

Lequeux *reads from his novel.* **Midgley** *looks over*
his shoulder and joins in.
During this **Cora** *can be seen putting on jewels from*
a jewel box (the metal container).

Lequeux	She came into my room
Lequeux	a woman whose face, although waxen
and	white, was eminently beautiful. Her
Midgley	paleness . . . She wore a brooch of rather
	uncommon pattern. It was a playing card,
	a tiny five of diamonds. At that moment
	the truth dawned . . . Quite undue alarm I
	decided. She said, 'Drink that, you'll feel
	better very quickly.' I gulped it down. It
	tasted very bitter but . . . Strange sharp
	pain which struck me across the eyes, a

	paralysis of the limbs and a feeling of giddiness . . . most deadly of poisons, insidious . . . I saw her in the air, in the clouds, everywhere; her voice rang in my ears; she was so lovely – yet so vile – a poisoner! . . . She knew secrets dead with the Borgias . . . She said 'Drink that.'
Crippen	I get ideas for novels. But I dont have a way with words, so if you just wrote them up. There's a man married to a termagant. He's in love with a beautiful and innocent girl who works as his secretary. He poisons his wife in the tea but he has drunk the tea himself without ill effect. How can this be? He drank an antidote first. The poison is indetectable. No suspicion falls on him. A perfect crime. He lives to an old age with his beloved. Does this idea appeal? I have many others. He kills his wife with poisoned gloves. / He –

Enter **Cora**.

Cora	Is everything ready, Hawley, my love? /	14
Crippen	Everything's ready, my love.	
Cora	The guests will be here any minute and nothing's ready.	
Crippen	Our most respected guests are already here.	
Cora	Enchanté, Mr Lequeux.	
Lequeux	Enchanté, Madame.	
Cora	(*to* **Crippen**) My friends, what about my friends, you've no respect / for them.	
Crippen	Respect, my love, I should think not, respect that tawdry / riff-raff, respect Bruce Miller,	
Cora	Tawdry.	
Crippen	a one man band, if I were cuckolded by a bank manager / I might have some respect or if he could play one single musical instrument to	
Midgley	What a charming brooch, Mrs Crippen.	
Cora	The rising sun. Do call me Belle.	
Crippen	a high professional standard.	
Cora	Professional standards? Forgive me laughing, my husband just made a joke.	

9

Crippen	Have you been to the music hall in London, Midgley?
Midgley	I'm looking forward to it.
Crippen	Cora will tell you which are the best acts.
Cora	Opera was my first ambition.
Midgley	Bit highbrow for me.
Cora	(*to* **Crippen**) Dont start on me about Bruce Miller. / What
Crippen	And the German students?
Cora	about your little typewriter? Ethel is a very dull name. It suits her.
Crippen	Belle is of course my wife's professional name. Her name is Cora. Or rather her name is Kunigunde, but that's rather a mouthful we find, Kunigunde Mackimotzki, Mackimotzki a Polish grocer, not quite the thing for top of the bill at the Empire Leicester Square, not that we've made the Empire Leicester Square yet but hope springs eternal, so she calls herself Belle Elmore, / you may have seen her name some way down the bill.
Cora	Dr Crippen is at the top of his profession. He'll send his diagnosis by mail order. Rhinitis Chronica Pharyngitis Eustachian Sulphingitis. The painless wonder. Cures for diseases that are incurable.
Midgley	We all have our dreams, Mrs Crippen. You're an artiste, your husband a physician. What higher callings? We all have our dreams, Belle.

Whist

More guests arrive, all music hall friends of **Cora's**. **Bruce Miller, Mr Martinetti, Mrs Smythson, Marie Lloyd**. *During the following* **Lequeux** *is making a play for* **Marie Lloyd**, **Cora** *is flirting with* **Bruce Miller**, **Crippen** *is standing apart.*

Mrs Smythson	Belle.
Cora	We're eight, that's two tables for whist.
Crippen	Count me out, my love.
Midgley	Do play, Crippen.
Smythson	Oh Dr Crippen, do play.
Cora	We can do very well without you.
Lequeux	I dont mind not playing.
Mrs Smythson	Oh Mr Lequeux, do play.
Midgley	We'll make one table and take turns. I need to watch, it's so long since I played.
Smythson	Oh Mr Midgley, do play.

They settle to playing.   22
First hand: **Cora, Miller, Lloyd, Martinetti.**
The others watch.

Midgley	What's the stake?
Smythson	Penny a quarter.
Lequeux	Wont break you.
Cora	(*to* **Crippen**) Are you going to stand there all the evening?
Lequeux	(*to* **Crippen**) Cards are a trivial way of passing the time. But I must confess a weakness. Ever since that night in Monte Carlo . . .
Cora	Oh what a hand.
Smythson	Dont say a word.
Midgley	Hearts are trumps.
Cora	Oh they are, they are.

They bid.   24

Lloyd	I propose.
Martinetti	Pass.
Cora	I accept. We ladies will show you.
Miller	Solo.
Cora	Solo, you devil.
Lloyd	Pass.
Martinetti	Misere.
Smythson *and* **Cora**	Misere!
Cora	Abondance. There.

Miller	Abondance in trumps.
Cora	Oh Mr Miller, you always have all the hearts.
Midgley	How many tricks does he have to make?
Cora	Are you looking at my hand, Mr Midgley?
Crippen	Just popping out for some air.
Midgley	Dont go. 26

Crippen *leaves. He goes to visit* **Ethel**. *Dance of coy tentative passion.*

Meanwhile, Evening at Hilldrop Crescent continues.

They play.

Smythson	He'll never make it.
Cora	Oh my best card.
Smythson	Dont say a word.
Lequeux	He's got to win this one.
All	Got you.

Martinetti *and* **Cora** *win last two tricks.* **Miller** *fails to make his bid.*

Cora	Two tricks down.
All	Pay up.
Lequeux	He had the ace.
Smythson	If you'd led the ten.
Midgley	Bold play, Belle.

Lequeux *pursues* **Marie Lloyd** *round the table and* 27 *similarly* **Cora** *pursues* **Miller**.

Lequeux	(*to* **Lloyd**) I sent you roses. I like your style.
Midgley	(*to* **Cora**) I like your style.
Cora	Unlucky at cards, lucky in love, Mr Miller.
Smythson	Oh Mr Midgley, do play.
Midgley	I will.
Smythson *and* **Midgley**	Oh Mr Lequeux, do play.

Second hand: **Midgley, Lequeux, Smythson,** 29

Lloyd *standing playing and repeating fragments of movement.*

Lequeux	Pass.
Smythson	I propose.
Lloyd	Pass.
Midgley	I accept.
Lequeux	Misere.
Smythson	Abondance.
Lloyd	Pass.
Midgley	Abondance in trumps.

The last round of bidding is repeated while **Cora** 30
tells **Miller** *she imagines herself singing opera and he dances seductively in front of her.*

Cora   I'm at La Scala. I'm gowned by Patou. I'm singing Medea. 'I have my revenge.'

The game continues.

Lequeux	Misere ouverte.
Smythson	Pass.
Lloyd	Pass.
Midgley	Abondance declaree.

Midgley *lays his cards on the table.*

All   Ooo!

Lequeux *again pursues* **Marie Lloyd**, *while* **Cora** 33
and **Smythson** *turn their attention to* **Midgley**.

Lequeux	(*to* **Marie Lloyd**) I had nothing. I sent you roses.
Cora	(*to* **Midgley**) You're a genius.
Smythson *and* **Midgley**	Beginner's luck.
Cora	Lucky at cards, lucky in love, Mr Midgley.
Lequeux	Wont you sing for us, Mrs Lloyd?
Smythson	Oh Mrs Lloyd, do sing.

Music Hall Song: 'She poisoned him, he poisoned her. They both took an antidote.'
Sally Owen and Michael Popper.
(Photo: Rosy Sanders)

| Midgley | Wont you sing for us, Mrs Crippen? Oh Belle, do sing. |

Music Hall Song

| | *Cora sings a music hall song. During the song* 35 *Marie Lloyd is doing a saucy dance with ribbons on sticks,* **Martinetti** *is doing funny faces and silly walks,* **Bruce Miller** *is doing a juggler-magician routine without props,* **Cora** *is doing a crass dance routine among them while she sings. She does it badly but is pleased with herself.* |

| Cora | There was a young lady in Paris,
    as history writers tell
Who poisoned her poor old father
    and both her brothers as well
She was pouring a bottle of poison
    adown of her husband's throat
When her lover says 'No dont bother'
    and gave him an antidote. |

She poisoned him, he poisoned her.
They both took an antidote.

He poisoned her, she poisoned him.
Oh! What a to-do.

| All | You cant trust 'em further than you can throw 'em. |

| | **Lloyd,** **Martinetti** *and* **Miller** *do a cod ballet* 38 *routine with* **Cora** *performing badly in the centre.* |

Smythson	Oh Belle, you've got no talent. I cant help admiring you.
Midgley	Oh Belle, you've got real talent. I cant help admiring you.
Lequeux	I'll never forget your magnificent performance. I cant help admiring you though you spurned my roses.

15

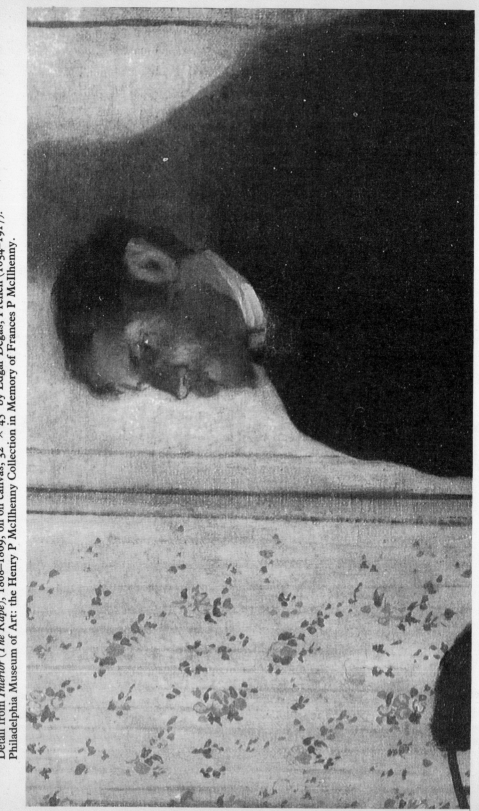

Detail from *Interior (The Rape)*, 1868–1869, oil on canvas, 32″ × 45″ by Edgar Degas, French (1834–1917). Philadelphia Museum of Art: the Henry P McIlhenny Collection in Memory of Frances P McIlhenny.

Cora *goes back to music hall song and others go*
back to previous material.

Cora   She poisoned him, he poisoned her,
                        She gave him an antidote.
                        Oh what a to-do.
                        Etc.

During this singing **Crippen** *finishes his dance with*
Ethel, *who remains on the floor, and enters Hilldrop*
Crescent. General embarrassment as the guests leave.

Cora's Death

Crippen *makes cocoa using a cup and spoon.* **Cora**
takes off her shoes, and her jewels, which she puts in
the box.

Cora   I wont sell my jewels so dont ask.
                        I like a lot of company and the house full
                            to suffocation, why not?
                        I won three-and-six, you can have that.
                        I should have gone misere.
Crippen   Drink your cocoa, my love, and we'll go to bed.
Cora   I want to be famous, I want the gentlemen
                        standing up to cheer and throwing flowers.
                        How's the little typewriter tonight?

Ethel *moves towards* **Crippen** *and nudges him with*
her head.

Crippen   Drink your cocoa, my love.
Cora   You're a nasty little quack with no soul.
                        I'm hoping to be on the bill with Marie
                            Lloyd.
                        The Music Hall Ladies Guild Ball – will
                            you try to enjoy it?
                        Mr Midgley's taken a fancy to me.

Cora *is getting sleepier.*

17

Cora's Death: 'Be quiet, someone will hear you.'
Pearce Quigley and Angela Tunstall.
(Photo: Robin Morris)

The **Chorus of Poisons** *singers appear above and*   43
start singing her to death and **Ethel** *starts a dance*   44
which refers to the fact that she may have suffered a
nervous breakdown and that on the evening of the
murder she kept putting curlers in hair again and
again and the landlady said 'You must relieve your
mind or you will go absolutely mad.' It's mostly
gestural with references to her hair and her ears and
spell casting. At the beginning her movements are
frantic and repetitive.

Cora   Remember the night I thought I was going
      to die?
      I said 'Wake up and get a priest, I'm going
      to die.'

Crippen *embraces* **Cora**.   45

Cora   And you took care of me.
Crippen Drink up your cocoa, my love, and we'll go to
bed.
Cora   Poor Belle's unlucky at cards and unlucky
      in love.
      They're all cheering me and throwing
      flowers.

Cora *is getting weaker. She seems to pass out in* 47
Crippen's *arms. Suddenly she screams and becomes*
frantic.   48
Crippen *moves away from her as she jerks up and*
crawls around the floor.
Ethel's *movements become calm.*

Cora   I'm going to die.
Crippen What's the matter, my love? Are you ill?

Cora *is trying to grab hold of* **Crippen**.   52

Cora   Help me. Take care of me. Make me
      better. Stop the pain.
Crippen Go to sleep, Cora, go to sleep.

Cora *and the* **Poisons** *go on shrieking while* **Ethel**

does a rapid triumph dance and **Crippen** *tries to restrain* **Cora.**

Crippen You're meant to go to sleep. It's not supposed to hurt. It's painless. Be quiet, someone will hear you. What are you doing? Hyoscine's meant to make you go to sleep. You're meant to die quietly, Cora, in your sleep.

Shrieking gets worse. **Crippen** *gets gun and shoots* **Cora,** *thus ending music.* **Ethel** *exits.* **Crippen** *disposes of the body by putting it out of sight behind the floor.*

Crippen *alone with his crime.*

Crippen When I was a child in Coldwater, Michigan, some nights I couldnt sleep and I crept downstairs. It seemed I was all alone in the house. How could I get away? How could I not be damned? I'd sit for hours by the stove trying to keep warm. The devil was always in the kitchen.

He remains sitting during the following scene.

Suspicion

Smythson *and* **Marie Lloyd** *try to get* **Inspector** 54
Dew *to take action.* **Dew** *has a book of missing persons.* **Midgley** *is with him. Meanwhile* **Ethel** *joins* **Crippen** *and is given* **Cora's** *brooch.*

Smythson Inspector Dew, my friend has disappeared.
Dew Hundreds of people vanish every day.
Smythson At first her husband said she'd gone away.
  And now he says she's dead just as I
    feared.

	That woman was seen trying on Belle's dresses.
	She came to the ball with Dr Crippen wearing Belle's rising sun brooch on her bosom.
	Belle never in a thousand years would have allowed another woman to wear her jewels.
Dew	(*meanwhile*) Wives often run away.
	Happens every day.
Smythson	My suspicions are becoming stronger in the direction of foul play.

Ethel *enters to* **Crippen,** *who reaches down to the*   56
body as if undressing it and gives **Ethel Cora**'s *dress*
and then her brooch, which he pins on **Ethel**.

Smythson	My friend has disappeared.
	She's dead just as I feared.
Midgley	I wonder where she's gone.
	I wonder why.

Marie Lloyd *moves in to observe* **Crippen** *and*   57
Ethel.

Smythson	There's no trace of her on the passenger lists.
	He doesnt even know what town she died in, he hasnt got a death certificate.
	He said she died at his son's house and his son wrote to say he knows nothing about it.
	My suspicions are becoming stronger in the direction of foul play.
Dew	Happens every day.

Dew *calls on* **Crippen**. **Ethel** *leaves*.   58

| **Dew** | I'd like to have a word with you about the death of your wife. |
| **Crippen** | Inspector Dew, I want to confess. I have lied. I lied when I said my wife was called away |

21

suddenly on family business. I lied when I said
she got pneumonia on the ship and the reason I
was so uncertain about the place of her death is
because the whole thing was a pack of lies. The
truth is my wife has left me. She's run off with
her lover, a prizefighter called Bruce Miller, who
has played here in music halls as a one man
band. I could not bear to be laughed at. She was
dead to me so I pretended she was dead. I have
to confess I also lied to Miss LeNeve, who now
lives with me as my wife, believing me a
widower. I am sorry to have wasted police time
by causing unnecessary suspicion. I tried to avoid
social embarrassment and have been punished by
being even more severely embarrassed.

Dew *moves away, satisfied.* **Crippen** *runs back to*   59
the body, which is still out of sight. His action   60
indicates that he chops the head off and puts it in a
hatbox (the metal container).

Dew	Hundreds of people vanish every day.
	Wives often run away. Happens every day.
Smythson	My suspicions are becoming stronger in
	the direction of foul play.
Midgley	Belle Elmore is a very charming woman.
	We're dull dogs. She wanted the bright
	lights.
Dew	Bright lights.
and	
Midgley	
Smythson	Foul play.

They all go off.

Ethel *runs in disguised as a boy. She is wearing a*
suit and carrying a hat. She dances with **Crippen.**
Her movements are stronger and more exuberant. It's
like a conversation between her movement and
Crippen'*s lines.*

Crippen   It is so precious a thought to me to tell you you

22

On the Ship: Cabalistic woman.

are always and ever my wifie and that not even death can come between us.

We have been so long one in heart, soul, thought and deed that, wifie darling, nothing can separate our inward consciousness and spirit.

No more sacred relations to each other such as ours could ever exist.

Crippen *puts on a false moustache.* **Ethel** *puts on the hat, tucking up her hair. She makes a move towards the hatbox,* **Crippen** *playfully forestalls her and takes the box with him as they run away.*

On the Ship

As they go off, **Captain Kendall** *and the* **Sailor** *appear on the deck of the ship.*
Ethel *and* **Crippen** *arrive with the hatbox.*

Crippen   Allow me to introduce myself. John Philo Robinson. My son. We are travelling abroad for his health. Owing to his delicate condition we require the exclusive use of a cabin for ourselves alone.

Midgley, Dew, Smythson *appear above and start* 61
to sing (see below). They are holding up plastic evidence bags containing hair, brooch, photograph.
Ethel *and* **Crippen** *are shown to their cabin.*
Kendall *is reading a newspaper.* **Ethel** *and* 62
Crippen *reappear on deck, look at the sea and fall* 63
asleep. **Kendall** *and* **Sailor** *retire but still watch the couple.*

All   Evidence.
Dew   There was one place in the house which
        held a peculiar fascination.

	I couldn't keep my mind from wandering back.
	A thrill of excitement.
	Evidence nauseatingly unmistakable.
	The putrified atmosphere.
	Wanted for Murder and Mutilation.
Smythson	What did I say? Foul play. Murder and Mutilation.
Midgley	I think there's been a mistake.
Dew	Traces of hyoscine hydrobromide.
Midgley	Hyoscine is a poison found in henbane or deadly nightshade, which commonly grows on waste ground. Sticky hairy leaves. Yellow and purple blossom. It is poisonous in all its parts. Hyoscine has a medical application for inducing twilight sleep.

*During the above, **Kendall** approaches the couple*   64
*and takes **Ethel**'s hat off so that her hair falls down.*
*He signals to the **Sailor**.*

Dew,	The message in the air
Smythson,	Racing over the sea.
Midgley	Ship pursuing ship pursuing ship . . .

*During the above the **Sailor** signals to **Marie Lloyd***   65
with flags and she in turn signals to the audience.
***Crippen** wakes briefly.*

| **Crippen** | (*to* **Kendall**) My son enjoyed the ship's concert last night. Forgive his not speaking, he is a little deaf and rather shy. |

***Crippen** goes back to sleep. Signalling continues.*   66
Kendall *replaces **Ethel**'s hair under her hat and*
*indicates to the **Sailor** to come and get the hatbox,*
*which **Crippen** is still holding. The **Sailor** struggles*   67
*with the sleeping **Crippen**, who finally wakes and*   68
snatches the box back.

| **Smythson** | If you'd listened to me they wouldnt have got away. |

25

On the Ship: 'Large pieces of human remains.' The Sailor attempts to get the hatbox from the sleeping Crippen. Left to right: Michele Smith, Pearce Quigley, Michael Popper (standing) and Stephen Goff. (Photo: Rosy Sanders)

On the Ship: Crippen, Ethel and the Dolphin dance. 'If you'd listened to me they wouldn't have got away.' Top: Michael O'Connor, Jackie Horner; middle: Michael Popper, Stephen Goff; bottom left: Michele Smith, Pearce Quigley. (Photo: Rosy Sanders)

Midgley	I think there's been a mistake. If they have run away it's to protect the reputation of Miss LeNeve and to start a new life.	

Crippen *watched by* **Kendall** *and the* **Sailor** 69
furtively drops the hatbox in the sea.

Dew	Large pieces of human remains No arms or legs and no head Removed the bones and the head.	

Kendall *and* **Sailor** *entertain* **Crippen** *and* **Ethel** 70
*with a curious dolphin dance, like formation
swimming, in which we can only see their legs upside
down.*

Dew	I cant keep my mind from the horror of
	    what I've seen
	The putrified atmosphere
	After this I'll never sleep the sleep of the
	    innocent.

Smythson	If you'd listened to me they wouldnt have got away The putrified atmosphere Hyoscine hydrobromide Everything points to his guilt.
Midgley	It's to protect the reputation of Miss LeNeve I think there's been a mistake Hyoscine hydrobromide I'm sure he's innocent.

Cora's *head appears over the edge of the ship.* 72
Crippen *recoils.*
Lloyd *does a triumphant flag dance.* 73
Kendall *and* **Sailor** *continue dolphin dance.*

Cora	You thought you'd thrown my head into
	    the sea
	You thought I'd fallen asleep
	I'm awake, I'm here, I'll never leave you
	    now
	I cant keep my mind from the horror

Cora	I want them throwing flowers
	Murder and mutilation
Smythson	Murder and mutilation
	The putrefied atmosphere
Midgley	He's one of the most agreeable men that I know
	The putrefied atmosphere
	Murder and mutilation
	Please say you're innocent
All	Murder and mutilation
	The death of your wife.
Crippen	We were like two children in the great unkind world who clung to one another and gave each other courage.

> **Kendall** *and the* **Sailor** *welcome* **Dew, Lloyd,**   74
> **Smythson** *and* **Midgley** *aboard the ship.* **Dew**   75
> *handcuffs* **Crippen**.
> **Lloyd, Kendall** *and* **Sailor** *do a triumphant dance.*   76

Dew	I arrest you for murder
	And then I'll grow flowers
	I cant keep my mind
Smythson	Murder and mutilation
	To mutilate your own wife
Midgley	You want to start a new life
	With the innocent you love.
	Your wife is magnificent
	I think there's been a mistake.
Cora	I'll never leave you now and you'll never escape me
	You thought I'd gone forever but I'll have my revenge

> *They all go off leaving* **Crippen** *and* **Ethel** *alone.*   78

Crippen	One Sunday how early I came for you and we had a whole day together which meant so much to us then. A rainy day but how happy we were with all sunshine in our hearts.

> *They embrace and walk slowly off watched by* **Cora**
> *who has transformed into* **Medea**.

29

Corinth: Medea: 'I want her dead.'   Angela Tunstall.   (Photo: Rosy Sanders)

Corinth

Medea   If I put my hand in fire   79
                             Would the pain rush out of my mind into
                                 my hand?
                             I could stand that.

                             Why my hand?
                             I want his hand on fire.
                             Her hand, I wouldnt feel a thing, I might
                                 still feel his hand.
                             I want her dead.
                             Set their house on fire.

Chorus of Poisons (*two singers and male dancer*)   80
assemble at the side with the metal box of poisons.   81
Dancer does gestural dance illustrating **Medea's**
words.

Medea   What and get caught?
                             Poison.
                             Poison that kills far away like the bite of a
                                 thought.
                             Wrap her body in fire.
                             Wrap fire round her head.

                             I could stop, I could leave, I could stop
                                 now.
                             She could live, he neednt grieve, I could
                                 go away.

                             But I have the power.
                             Poison that eases into her body out of my
                                 mind.
                             The pain will burn her body and leave my
                                 mind cold.
                             The horror will rush out of my mind.

Midgley *and* **Jason** *enter as* **Medea** *and* **Poisons**   83
go off.

31

Midgley	Today we've something to celebrate.
Jason	What? / You've heard – ah, sorry.
Midgley	You know the knock problem – what?
Jason	Nothing, go on, yes, the knock in car engines.
Midgley	I tried everything from ethyl acetate and aluminum fluoride to camphor and melted butter. Thirty thousand chemical compounds.
Jason	Like those endless days at sea.
Midgley	I thought this could take my entire life.
Jason	You think you're going to fall off the world.
Midgley	You get one that works and it stinks of garlic.
Jason	Wave after bloody wave, you want to give up.
Midgley	But then I took a look at the periodic table and, wait for it, everything that was nearly okay was clustered down the bottom. That was like you killing the serpent.
Jason	And you struck gold.
Midgley	What I've struck is lead. Lead in the gas stops the knock.
Jason	You'll make your fortune.
Midgley	A golden fleece. And leaded gas. So we both have something to celebrate, I guess.
Jason	I do have something to celebrate. I'm getting married.
Midgley	I always thought you and Medea were already – congratulations. We'll have a party.
Jason	Not to Medea. / We did go through a form of
Midgley	Not to Medea?
Jason	marriage but it's not legal here.
Midgley	What?
Jason	To Creusa. The princess?
Midgley	My god, has Medea left you? Dont do anything rash. She'll come back. This is terrible. Shall I speak to her for you?
Jason	No. No, thank you, no. She hasnt left me.
Midgley	What? For Creusa? You're out of your mind. Medea's – there's no comparison.
Jason	Maybe you can comfort her.
Midgley	She wouldnt look at me – what are you saying?
Jason	No, I mean cheer her up, stop her being angry with me.
Midgley	She shouldnt be angry?
Jason	Look, Midgley, you dont live with her. She was

32

	wonderful in her own country, dealing with monsters, I owe her a lot. But when you get back to civilisation. Not everyone's as tolerant as you.	
Midgley	And Creusa's father is King of Corinth.	
Jason	She's beautiful, Midgley. And her father's King of Corinth.	
Midgley	It's a career move.	
Jason	It's a brilliant career move. I'm a hero, I can have what I like. But it wont last. Poor old Jason, always going on about his golden fleece, crazy wife.	
Midgley	I thought you loved her.	
Jason	Get a grip, Midgley. When the King dies I'll run Corinth. Would you give up your leaded petrol? Help me talk her round. She likes you.	
Midgley	Does she? Has she said so?	

Enter **Medea**.

Medea	I deceived my father for you. I murdered my brother. I betrayed my country and helped you steal its treasure. / I'm sorry	84
Jason	Medea, I do appreciate . . .	
Medea	that's not enough. I'm sorry I didnt have a sister / so I could drink her blood.	
Jason	I never suggested . . .	
Midgley	Medea, listen.	
Medea	Jason, when you think of all she's done. If I could go home to a time before I knew you.	
Jason	When I say I'm going to marry the princess . . . Marriage doesnt mean much here. Wives are a matter of career. Passion is for a mistress. We've turned up in Corinth with nothing except that I'm a hero. We've a chance to get in with the royal family. I'm doing it for you. I'll buy you a house.	
Midgley	(*to* **Medea**) Wives are a matter of career. Passion. A house. (*to* **Jason**.) This is terrible.	
Medea	Without you I'd be a princess. Without me you'd be dead. Jason's a hero.	85

33

	Who saved you? Who poisoned the serpent? Who got the golden fleece?
Midgley	Is this true?
Medea	Medea's the hero.

She repeats this through **Jason**'s *next speech, and* **Midgley** *joins in.*

Jason	You were nobody. You were desperate to get out of that godforsaken country. If you'd stayed there no one would ever have heard of you, you're only famous for helping me.
Medea	The King should give me his daughter and let me rule over Corinth.
Midgley	I cant stand this. Two people who are so magnificent.
Jason	Marriage doesnt mean much here.
Midgley	She gave up everything.
Medea	I murdered my brother.
Jason	This is our chance to be rich and powerful.
Midgley	She's already made you rich and powerful.
Medea	I'll have my revenge.
Jason	I'll buy you a house.
Midgley	But she's magnificent.
Medea	Tell me about the house. Tell me murder's good. Make me hate you more.
Midgley	I cant defend him. I'm sorry. You're the most extraordinary woman. Try not to hate him. Things may turn out for the best, you have to keep on and sometimes things suddenly . . . I wish I could put things right.

The singer **Poisons** *enter and begin preparing the*   86
poison dress, taking poisons from the box.

Medea	(*to* **Midgley**) If only I'd loved a man like you. I'd be famous for sweetness. I hate this rage. I'm the same Medea who cures the sick and brings the dead to life. I'll believe he's marrying her to make me happy. I'll live in his house.

| Medea | Take this dress and crown to the princess. |

As **Medea** *gives dress to* **Midgley**, **Creon** *and*   90
Creusa *appear above.* **Creusa** *starts to descend.*

Medea	Tell her it comes from a great enchantress.
	Tell her it's woven with spells for her
	happiness.
Midgley	Things have turned out for the best. You
	have to keep on and sometimes things
	suddenly . . . Today we have something to
	celebrate.

Jason *and* **Medea** *go off together.*   91
Creusa *has arrived at the top of a steep slope.*
Midgley *takes the dress to* **Creusa.**
Everyone watches in silence as she puts the dress on.
Medea *returns to watch.*

Death of Creusa and Creon

All the **Poisons** *go to* **Creusa.**   92
Singing **Poisons**, **Medea** *and* **Midgley** *begin to*
sing her to death.
Creusa *begins to feel the effects.*
One of the singing **Poisons** *does an incantation over*   94
her.   95
The **Singers** *move away with* **Medea,** *leaving*
Creusa *with the dancing* **Poisons.**
Creon *watches from above.*
Midgley *is watching from the side.*
Singers *prod* **Creusa.**   97
Dancers *move around her as she suffers, jumping*   98
over her, dancing with her and pushing her from one
to the other.
Creusa *is crawling on the floor in agony. She rolls*   100
off the floor, runs and falls dead.   101
    102
Creon *descends to* **Creusa,** *he clasps her in his arms* 103
and becomes glued to her body and dies.

35

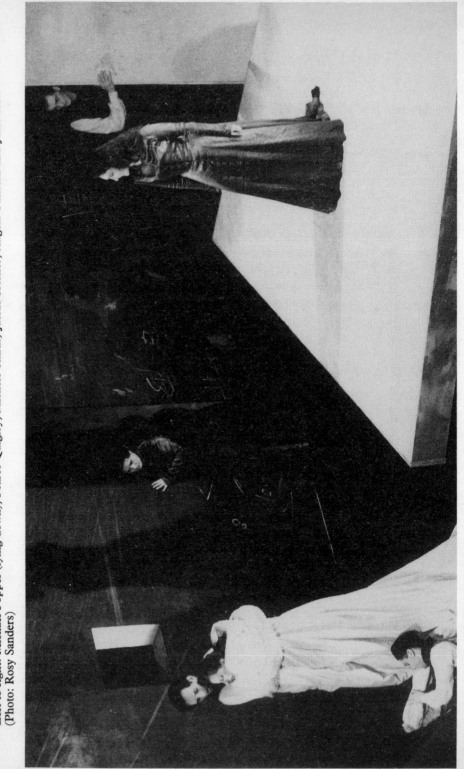

Medea's Triumph: 'Yes, I can bring the dead to life. But not for you.'
Left to right: Michael Popper (lying down), Pearce Quigley, Michele Smith, Jackie Horner, Angela Tunstall and Józic Koc.
(Photo: Rosy Sanders)

> **Poisons** *and* **Medea** *do a triumphant dance.* 104
> **Midgley** *is watching with horror.*

Lament for Creusa

> **Dancers** *lay out large white sheet and lay* **Creusa** 111
> *in it.*
> **Jason** *enters and grieves over her body. She is put in* 113
> *his arms wrapped in the sheet and* **Creon** *is placed* 114
> *at her feet.*

Chorus O nuit désastreuse, o nuit effroyable, où retente tout à coup comme un éclat de tonnerre cette étonnante nouvelle: Madame se meurt, Madame est morte. Madame est passé du matin au soir ainsi que l'herbe du champ. Le matin elle fleurissait, avec quelle grâce, vous le savez; le soir nous la vîmes séchée. Quelle diligence! En neuf heures, l'ouvrage est accompli.

Midgley I didnt know. I thought I was putting things right. If I could go back to this morning.

Medea's Triumph

> **Medea** *sings triumphantly at* **Jason**, *who circles* 115
> *aimlessly with the wrapped body of* **Creusa** *in his*
> *arms.*

Medea Yes I can bring the dead to life. But not
for you.
It's no thrill healing, I'd rather kill.

A man thinks he's drunk. He's dead.

37

Medea   His skin shrivels, his eyes are hollow, his
           hair goes white, his teeth break like
           glass.
        Secret de crapaud. Venin de crapaud.
        Breath, bite, urine and excrement
        Crushed in a mortar and left to putrefy.
        Poison from moles, pigeons, fish and
           snakes,
        Poison from hanged men and suicides.

        I love this rage.
        How her body melted from its bones.
        You thought I'd gone forever but I have
           my revenge.

Creusa *and* **Creon** *dissolve out of the scene.* 118
The two dancing **Poisons** *briefly become dragons* 119
around **Medea.**

Medea   My enemies melted in fire
        Your palace on fire
        Now I'm flying in fire where you cant
           come, in the fiery air on the wings of
           dragons.

Medea *goes off with the dragons.*

Jason *and* **Midgley** *shattered*

Jason   I should have known. / Why did I ever get
Midgley   You couldnt have known.
Jason   involved with her? She's a maniac. Someone who
        killed her own brother, I should have known, / I
Midgley   I should have known. I shouldnt have taken the
        dress.
Jason   should never have brought her back with me, I
        was obsessed – you couldnt have known.
Midgley   Things dont always turn out the way you think.
        Impossibly horrible things sometimes happen and
        that's what's happened here. We have to keep
        going. You've got to run Corinth. I've got work
        to do.

Jason   I cant keep my mind from the horror.

Poisons (*two singers, female dancer*) *assemble with*   120
box of poisons, putting labels on bottles.
Midgley *comforts* **Jason.**

Midgley   I've had a new idea, try and listen. It's to
keep things cool. Fish and meat and milk
so they wont putrefy in hot weather and
make people sick. The common refrigerant
is ammonia, which is harmful.

Dancing **Poison** *begins sinuous suggestive dance.*   121

Midgley   By using the periodic table I hit on this in
only three days. Dichlorodifluoromethane,
we've called it freon, a type of CFC. I took
some in my mouth to show it wasnt
poison, blew on a flame and it went out.

Midgley *and* **Jason** *go off as* **Brinvilliers** (**Medea**)
enters and the **Poisons** *hold out the box of poisons to*
her.

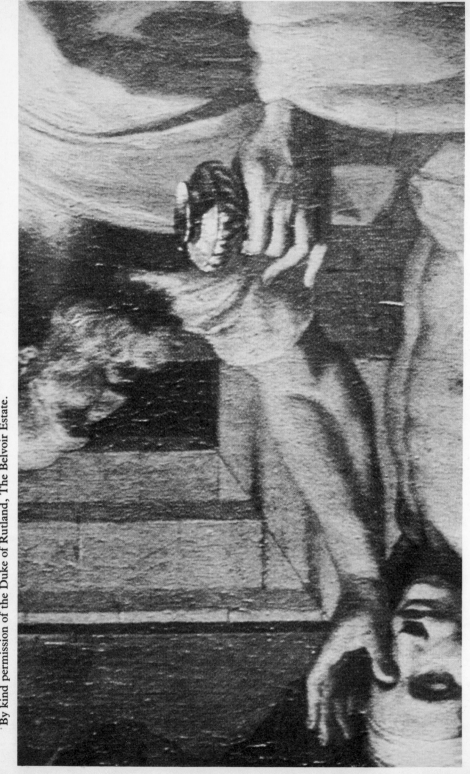

Detail from *Extreme Unction* by Nicholas Poussin (Picture Gallery) (c) English Life Publications Ltd. By kind permission of the Duke of Rutland, The Belvoir Estate.

Hospital

Medea *is now* **Mme de Brinvilliers**. *She is in the hospital. 'Many of the ladies of Paris faithfully visited the sick . . . Brinvilliers was allowed to wander at will. She brought and administered sweets, wine and biscuits . . . patients who received gifts from her hands invariably died in greatest agony . . . Beds built to contain two patients were crowded with six.' (Mme de Brinvilliers and her times by H Stokes, pub. Lane, London, 11 September 1912.)*

The sick are the four dancers, including **Creusa**. 125 *They enter and get under a large sheet.* **Brinvilliers** *gives medicine to the sick, assisted by the singing* **Poisons**, *and one by one they die, using movements reminiscent of the music hall characters. They are lowered behind the floor, as* **Cora's** *body was.*

Brinvilliers

Healing you I hurt you
Curing you I kill you
Secrets of life and new death.
Poisons that kill
Fill your blood fill your breath.
By my skill
I heal you and bring a new death.

Brinvilliers *goes.*

Laboratory

Sainte-Croix, Exili *and* **La Chausee** *appear in the* 128 *laboratory.* **Exili** *and* **La Chaussee** *are bottling poisons.* **Sainte-Croix** *is checking orders.* **Creusa** *takes her dress off, becoming* **Mme Sainte-Croix**, *and exits.*

Exili	Our new product will be so delicate
	One breath will be fatal
	The greatest art is indetectable
	We'll corner the market.
Sainte-Croix	We've orders from Hamburg, Venice and Madrid.
Exili	The death seems natural
	A little blood coagulates in the heart.
	Our fame is to be unknown
	The poison is imperceptible
Sainte-Croix	This is the one that's going to make our fortune.
Exili	To simulate a slow decline
	An emanation in the air
	We'll corner the market.

Midgley *joins them.*

Sainte-Croix	This is Signor Exili, the cleverest man in the world. Mr Midgley, whom I'm lucky enough to have as my children's tutor. A great chemist, a great alchemist. You find us as usual in search of the philosopher's stone and the elixir of life.
Exili	Philosopher's stone. Elixir of life. Great ambitions.
Midgley	Lead into gold. Eternal youth. Great ambitions.
Exili	Do you know the elixirs of Paracelsus?
Midgley	Not very well.
Exili	Primum Ens Melissae.
	Dissolve a phial of potassium carbonate
	Macerate leaves of the melissa plant
	Pour on absolute alcohol.
	Collect, distil, evaporate to the thickness of a syrup.

Primum Ens Sanguinis.
Blood from the vein of a healthy young person.
Digest with twice the amount of alcahest
Caustic lime and absolute alcohol
Distilled ten times and set on fire.
Separate filter preserve the red liquid.

Midgley *echoes what he's told, jumps ahead with a*

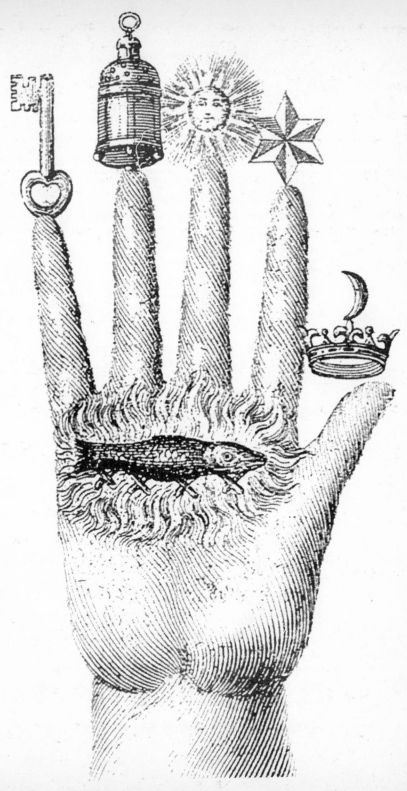

On the Ship: Medea: The hand.

bit he remembers, gets something wrong, joins in enthusiastically.

Midgley	People must say to you what they say to me, Wild goose chase. But we dont listen.
Sainte-Croix	Mr Midgley stops things putrifying by keeping them cold.
Midgley	And the CFCs also have an application in air conditioning.
Exili	An emanation in the air?
Midgley	I tested them on rats, and they're completely non-toxic.
Exili	And now if you'll excuse us.
Midgley	May I watch?

Sainte-Croix *and* **Exili** *are moving up to the laboratory.*

Sainte-Croix	Unfortunately we're working with dangerous chemicals and we have to wear masks.
Midgley	Do you have a spare mask?

Sainte-Croix *and* **Exili** *put on their masks and start work.*

Midgley	Best of luck then.

Midgley *goes.*

Sainte-Croix	Does he know?
Exili	He doesnt know.
Sainte-Croix	He knows.

They turn back to their work.   133

Meanwhile **Mmes de Brinvilliers, de Sevigne, Sainte-Croix** *and* **Dufay** *are doing their toilette.* **M de Brinvilliers** *is lying ill at* **Brinvilliers'** *feet, being fed poisoned wine,* **Mme Sainte-Croix** *is massaging* **de Sevigne, Dufay** *is powdering herself and clouds of powder rise into the air.*

Midgley *reappears above at the side.*

Laboratory: 'You do nothing. The days pass. You grow old. You die.'
Top: Stephen Goff and Józic Koc. Left to right bottom: Michele Smith
behind Jackie Horner, Angela Tunstall, Michael Popper (lying down),
Sally Owen. (Photo: Rosy Sanders)

Exili	To simulate a slow decline
	An emanation in the air
	We'll corner the market.
Midgley	(*to himself*) Something strange is going on here.
	There's something in the air.
Sevigne	What rubbish do we rub on our faces?
	Fat boiled up from the feet of a sheep.
	Why do we make our heads look like cabbages?
	The most ridiculous thing we can devise.
	Why do we stick black patches on our faces
	And call them flies?
	Why do we spend half the day asleep?
Sevigne *and* Brinvilliers	You do nothing. The days pass. You grow old. You die.

Mmes Sainte-Croix *and* **Dufay** *have gone into a   135
face massage dance.*

Hoca

136

Evening at the **de Brinvilliers'***. La Chaussee,
with wine goblets, leaps onto the gaming table.* **Exili**
*is the dealer for the game of Hoca. He has cards and
a croupier's rake. Everyone from the previous scene
is there. They all have money.*

*Hoca is played by having a table divided into
numbered compartments. Player puts stake, banker
draws a numbered card and pays 28 × stake.*

*Behavour throughout this scene is sexy, bitchy and
increasingly savage.* **Dufay** *is the mistress of the*
Marquis de Brinvilliers. **Sainte-Croix** *is the lover
of* **Mme de Brinvilliers**. *She keeps an eye on the*
Marquis, *who plays heavily and loses.* **Mme**

46

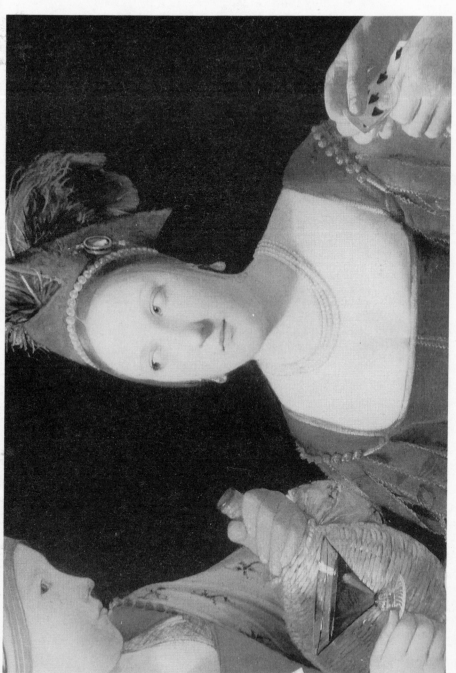

Detail from *The Cheat with the Ace of Clubs*, about 1630, oil on canvas, 97.8 × 156.2cm. by Georges de la Tour, French (1593–1652). Kimbell Art Museum, Fort Worth, Texas.

Sainte-Croix watches **Sainte-Croix** *jealously.*
Midgley *is new to the game. He is increasingly
infatuated with* **Mme de Brinvilliers.** **La
Chaussee** *serves wine, helps* **Sainte-Croix** *and*
Exili *cheat and, as the evening gets wilder, makes
rough passes at* **Dufay.** *De Sevigne is flirtatious
and observant, explaining things to* **Midgley.** *The
dancers often break into phrases of movement.
Because the* **Marquis de Brinvilliers** *has been
poisoned, his movements are deliberate, jerky and
unsteady.*

Brinvilliers	Shall we play
	Hoca, lansequenet, portique, basset,
	ombre?
Others	Ombre, basset, portique, lansequenet,
	hoca?
	Hoca, hoca.

They place bets. The first game.   137

	The most dangerous game
	Banned in Italy
	Two popes have forbidden the faithful to
	play
	Parliament wants to ban it
	Magistrates want to ban it
	Six trade guilds want to ban it
	Hoca.
Sevigne	The mere rumour it's going to be
	fashionable has given rise to an infinity of
	tables.
All	Hoca.
Midgley	What's so dangerous about hoca?
Sainte-Croix	There's so many ways of cheating.
Midgley	Arent you playing?
Sainte-Croix	I've given up. I taught Exili all I knew about
	gambling and he taught me all he knew.
Midgley	About?
Sainte-Croix	All he knew.

Dufay *has won the first game.*   139

Hoca: Left to right: Stephen Goff, Sally Owen, Michele Smith, Michael Popper (kneeling), Jackie Horner (front), Józic Koc (back centre), Pearce Quigley (back right), Angela Tunstall (front right). (Photo: Rosy Sanders)

Exili	Thirty-two paying thirty-two, a stake of twenty écus pays five hundred and sixty. Faites vos jeux.

Placing bets for second game.　　　　　140

Sevigne	Dangerous game.
Midgley	Do I dare play?
Sainte-Croix	Madame de Montespan lost half a million and won it back on three cards.
Brinvilliers	(*to* **Midgley**) You could learn a lot from Sainte-Croix.
	(*to* **Marquis**) No good at cards are you, my love?
	(*to* **Midgley**) He's lost two fortunes, his and mine.
Exili	Rien ne va plus.
Others	Hoca.

Midgley *wins the second game.*　　　　　142

Exili	Nine paying nine. Ten écus is two hundred and eighty.
Midgley	I won, I won. I won all that? This is amazing.
Brinvilliers	Lost again, my love?

Mme de Brinvilliers *and the* **Marquis** *quarrel –*　143
she sings, he dances.

Brinvilliers	You've lost two fortunes, cant you stop?
	You'll give whatever you win to Madame Dufay.
	At least Sainte-Croix knows how to play cards.

Meanwhile, bets for third game.

Exili	Faites vos jeux.
Midgley	Do I dare play?
Sevigne	He cant stop.
	Expensive mistress.

Sainte-Croix corrects the cards.

Exili	Rien ne va plus.
Others	Hoca.

Midgley *wins the third game.*   144

Midgley	I won. I won again. This is amazing.
Sevigne	The Marquis de Brinvilliers has lost five
and	thousand.
Exili	
Sainte-Croix	(*to* **Mme Sainte-Croix**) No of course I'm not still in love with Madame de Brinvilliers. The woman's a monster.

She goes to place a bet. Fourth game.   145

Exili	Faites vos jeux.

Sainte-Croix *joins* **Mme de Brinvilliers.**

Brinvilliers	Beloved, why havent I killed that man?
	I dont know how I've lived with him so
	long.
	I wish you hadnt married that plain girl.
Sainte-Croix	You know marriage doesnt mean anything.
	Wives are a career. Her dowry paid for the
	laboratory.
Brinvilliers	I dont like her.
Sevigne	That poor girl.
	Her dowry paid.
All	Hoca.

Midgley *wins fourth game.*   147

Midgley	I've won again, this is amazing.
Sevigne	The Marquis de Brinvilliers has lost ten
and	thousand.
Exili	

Brinvilliers *goes to* **Midgley.**   148
Mme Sainte-Croix *goes to* **Sainte-Croix** *and slaps his face.*

Brinvilliers	Lucky at cards, lucky in love, Monsieur Midgley.
Midgley	Lucky? After what you made me do?
Brinvilliers	I know you will always look after my interests.
	That stupid man is quite incapable.
	I dont know how I've lived with him so long.
	If only I'd married a man like you.
Sevigne	That poor man.
	Quite incapable.

Sainte-Croix *beckons* **La Chaussee** *and secretly* 150
gives him a card, which he takes to **Exili.**

Sainte-Croix	(*to* **Mme Sainte-Croix**) I've taught Exili how to play hoca. Put your stake on eighteen.

She places her stake. Fifth game. 151

Brinvilliers *and* **Marquis** *quarrel.*

Brinvilliers	Cant you stop?
	This is my money.
	Correct the cards.
Midgley	Extraordinary woman.
and	
Sevigne	

Brinvilliers *joins* **Sainte-Croix.** 153
Midgley *is counting his winnings.*

Sainte-Croix	Have you been to the hospital?
Brinvilliers	Twelve doses of weakest solution
	Cant see or speak
	The boy has a strong constitution
	His skin shrivels, his eyes are hollow, his teeth break like glass
	But he wont die.
	Venin de crapaud
	Ruptoire that pierces
	Hyoscine.
Exili	Rien ne va plus.

52

Others	Hoca
Exili	Paying number eighteen.

Mme Sainte-Croix *has won the fifth game.* 155

Sevigne	The Marquis de Brinvilliers has lost fifteen
and	thousand.
Exili	

Sevigne *joins* **Midgley** *again while others place bets* 156
for sixth game.

Sevigne	Sainte-Croix taught Exili to play hoca.
Midgley	How do you mean?
Sevigne	And Exili taught Sainte-Croix . . .
Midgley	What? What?
Sevigne	Signor Exili had to leave Italy.
	He was employed by the great.
Midgley	To do what?

She whispers to him. (We hear **Brinvilliers** *who is* 157
still singing about poisons with **Sainte-Croix**).

Sevigne	Didnt you know?
Midgley	I dont want to know.
Sevigne	Didnt you know?
Midgley	Does she know?
Sevigne	I warn you not to give way to her caresses.
	They're full of danger.
Midgley	Yes I know. But I dont want to know. I'm
	enchanted.

Meanwhile.

Brinvilliers	Venin de crapaud
	Ruptoire that pierces
	Hyoscine.
Exili	Rien ne va plus.
Others	Hoca.

Mme de Sainte-Croix *wins the sixth game.* 159

53

Sevigne *and* **Exili**	The Marquis de Brinvilliers has lost twenty thousand.

Brinvilliers *attacks* **Marquis** *again, they quarrel*   160
furiously. He is unsteady from being poisoned.

Brinvilliers	This is my money . . . I was only seventeen . . . your dissipation . . . any woman of spirit . . . my own fortune . . . go on, lose some more, faites vos jeux . . . rien ne va plus.

Meanwhile **Sevigne** *is still warning* **Midgley**.

Sevigne	I warn you Her caresses are full of danger.
Midgley	I dont want to know. I'm enchanted.

Sainte-Croix *seeing the* **Marquis** *has been poisoned* 162
goes to **Brinvilliers**.

Sainte-Croix	What have you given him?
Brinvilliers	Venin de crapaud. A slow decline. Beloved. Get rid of that plain girl and marry me.
Sainte-Croix	Beloved.
Brinvilliers	Beloved.

Exili *has handed over the bank to* **La Chaussee**   163
and come forward. **Sainte-Croix** *goes to him.*

Sainte-Croix	She's giving her husband poison. I dont want to marry her. We've already had a long and terrible life. Give me some antidote.
Exili	Theriac? Orvietu?

They give antidote to the **Marquis**.   164

The seventh game. **Midgley** *goes to* **Brinvilliers**.   165

Midgley	I'm staking all my winnings.

They both place bets. So do **Exili** *and the* **Marquis.**
Dufay *and* **Mme Sainte-Croix** *dance wildly.*

Midgley	Let me save you.
	Let me take you away.

Sainte-Croix *and* **Exili** *are fixing the game.*　　　166

Sevigne	I warn you
	Her caresses are full of danger.
Brinvilliers	Save me?
	It's I who have the power.
	I poisoned my father,
	A slow decline.
	I poisoned my brothers.
Midgley	(*meanwhile*) Please dont tell me.
	Let me take you away.
Brinvilliers	Save me?
	Who's going to hurt me?
	I killed my father
	I killed my brothers
	It's I who have the power
Midgley	(*meanwhile*) Please dont tell me.
	I'm enchanted.
All	Hoca.

La Chausee *holds up the winning number.*　　　168
Everyone moves onto the table.
Disappointment, as all go 'Ahhh'.
Exili *has won all the money with the seventh game.*

Sevigne	Exili won a fortune on one card.

La Chausee, Sainte-Croix *and* **Exili** *are sharing*　169
out the money. **Mmes Sainte-Croix, Dufay** *and* **de**
Sevigne *are preparing to go.* **Sevigne** *flirts with*
Exili *now that he has won.*

Midgley	I staked all my winnings and I lost.
Exili	Rien ne va plus.

As they leave, **Brinvilliers** *takes* **Sainte-Croix** *aside.*170

Brinvilliers	I told him.
Sainte-Croix	Why?
Brinvilliers	He adores me.
Sainte-Croix	Not enough. We'll have to get rid of him. Ask him to come to your room.

Sainte-Croix *leaves.* **Brinvilliers** *and* **Midgley** *are* 171 *alone.*

Brinvilliers	Come to my room at midnight.
Brinvilliers *and* **Midgley**	I'm in your power.

Midgley *goes.*
Brinvilliers *stays as the scene changes to her bedroom.*

Assignation

Sainte-Croix *joins* **Brinvilliers**. *He brings her the box of poisons and then starts to spread a sheet.* **Midgley** *watches them from above through a window.* **Sainte-Croix** *leads* **Brinvilliers** *to the bed, and taking a knife hides in the room.*

Midgley

Why? Why? Is he there to watch us make 172
  love?
I know that should stop me but do I care?
Is he there to kill me?
Let me just see her and see if I stay with
  her
Let me just breathe the same air.
Maybe I dont care if I die.

Midgley *goes into* **Brinvilliers'** *room. She woos him* 175 *but he is unresponsive.*

Brinvilliers

Come in my sweet. Your hands are cold.
Why wont you look at me? You seem so

56

sad. You're the most extraordinary man. If only I'd married a man like you.

They kiss. **Midgley** *breaks away.*

Midgley Why do you want to kill me?

Brinvilliers *catches him by the throat.* **Sainte-Croix** *jumps out, scuffle,* **Sainte-Croix** *runs away.* **Brinvilliers** *rushes to the box and tries to take poison.* **Midgley** *stops her. She wraps herself in the sheet.*

Brinvilliers I want to die.

They sit exhausted all night.   176

Midgley Dont kill yourself.
Brinvilliers Dont leave me.
Midgley Dont kill me.
Brinvilliers Dont betray me.

By the end **Midgley** *has moved to her and lies down beside her. She sleeps. He covers her with his coat. It is morning.*

Morning After

Sainte-Croix *comes in with a cup of coffee. He offers it to* **Midgley,** *who shakes his head,* **Sainte-Croix** *takes a sip himself and offers it again to* **Midgley,** *who drinks. They share the coffee while they talk.*

Midgley How am I supposed to feel?

Sainte-Croix *shrugs.*

You tried to kill me.

Sainte-Croix	That was last night.
Midgley	And what? This morning, what?
Sainte-Croix	You want me to stab you? You want me to cry and kiss you?

They drink some coffee.

There's a middle-aged couple called Brunet, quite rich, musical, they get a famous flautist to play at their parties and Madame becomes his mistress. But, meanwhile, Monsieur is arranging for the musician to marry the daughter. Invitations go out, Madame's wild with jealousy, and she poisons her husband. So what should the young man do? Everyone advises him to switch brides and marry the widow, he gets rich quicker, and the king was at the wedding.

You know Madame de Dreux? Wife of the politician? She's not 30 and she's poisoned three lovers. She did get caught but she just got a little fine and society finds her divinely amusing. Women wont sit next to her latest lover at dinner in case he smiles at them.

Midgley	Dont people get punished?
Sainte-Croix	Only if you've no connections. And I'll tell you another funny thing, the executioner is reliably reported to have poisoned his own wife. Come on, Midgley. And it's not just love affairs. The whole political life of the country depends on poison. Richelieu kept cats to smell his food. Colbert is constantly ill. Everyone in public life drinks antidote every morning. So of course it's a constant challenge. Exili and I are working on something imperceptible, one breath is fatal. People want this, Midgley, we've buyers all over Europe. We'll make a fortune.
Midgley	No.
Sainte-Croix	I dont want to kill you, Midgley. If you cant be friends you'd better go away.
Midgley	I keep thinking I should go home. I could be on a ship. But I cant leave her.
Sainte-Croix	Then you're in it with us, arent you? Dont

	worry. Everything's pointless anyway. People are vile. Death doesnt matter.
Midgley	I'm in love.

They sit in silence.

	I cant keep awake. Did you give me something?
Sainte-Croix	No, you're tired.
Midgley	It's delicious.

Midgley *sleeps*.

Breakfast

Sainte-Croix *carefully wakes* **Brinvilliers** *and gives her coffee.*

Brinvilliers	I thought you'd run away.	179
Sainte-Croix	You wish I'd killed him?	
Brinvilliers	If someone looks at you, you run away.	
Sainte-Croix	You want me to kill him?	
Brinvilliers	I wish I was waking up into a day that wasnt already spoiled.	
Sainte-Croix	You started this.	
Brinvilliers	You taught me poison.	
Sainte-Croix	You told me who to kill.	
Brinvilliers	We killed them for you.	
Sainte-Croix	So you could get money.	
Brinvilliers	So you could get my money.	
Sainte-Croix	And for revenge.	

Pause.

Brinvilliers	Do you love me?
Sainte-Croix	Why ask?

Pause.

Sainte-Croix	On the one hand you're sick of what we do. On

	the other hand you're trying to kill your husband.
Brinvilliers	You gave him antidote to save him.
Sainte-Croix	I wont marry you.

Pause.

Brinvilliers	I've been giving you poison too.
Sainte-Croix	I told you you hated me.
Brinvilliers	It may be to kill you. It may just be to reach inside your body.

Pause.

Sainte-Croix	Do you think I didn't know? I'm hard to poison, I know the antidotes. And why do you think you feel so ill and sad? Remorse? A little drop of remorse in your coffee.
Brinvilliers	I know what you give me. I can save myself. I know everything you know.
Sainte-Croix	Do we go on like this till we die of old age?
Brinvilliers	I wish I could wake up.

They sit in silence.
Sainte-Croix *gets up.*

Brinvilliers	Where are you going?
Sainte-Croix	To work.
Brinvilliers	I feel worse when I'm alone.

Sainte-Croix *goes.*

Death of Sainte-Croix

Sainte-Croix *goes off and appears above in laboratory.* **Mme Sainte-Croix** *comes to him and they embrace;* **Brinvilliers** *sees them and leaves.* **Sainte-Croix** *puts on glass mask and starts to work. The two dancing* **Poisons** *appear. One of them*

takes off his mask and the other breathes into his
mouth, poisoning him. He staggers out of the
laboratory breathing painfully and noisily, while
they watch. While grabbing the box to find an
antidote he collapses on the floor. **Mme Sainte-**
Croix *runs in and he dies at her feet.*

The Casket

Mme de Brinvilliers *arrives to confront* **Mme**   180
Sainte-Croix. Mme Sainte-Croix *wont give up*
the casket (box of poisons). **Desgrez** *arrives,*   181
discovers the body and the casket and examines the
blood on the wall, the knife and the sheet.

Brinvilliers	I've come to offer my condolences on your husband's unfortunate accident. I've come to collect a casket which is my property and concerns me alone.
Desgrez	Mysterious circumstances Impound all documents Everything is in the custody of the law.

Midgley *wakes up and sees* **Sainte-Croix'** *stiff*   182
body being taken away by **La Chaussee. Sevigne**
and **Dufay** *arrive.*

Midgley	My poor friend.
Sevigne	Another scandal.

Mme Sainte-Croix *gives the casket to* **Desgrez.**   183
He opens the casket and takes out what he finds.

Desgrez	Letters. A number of powders, liquid clear as water. Letters from Madame de Brinvilliers.

Dufay *and* **Sevigne** *are reading the letters while*

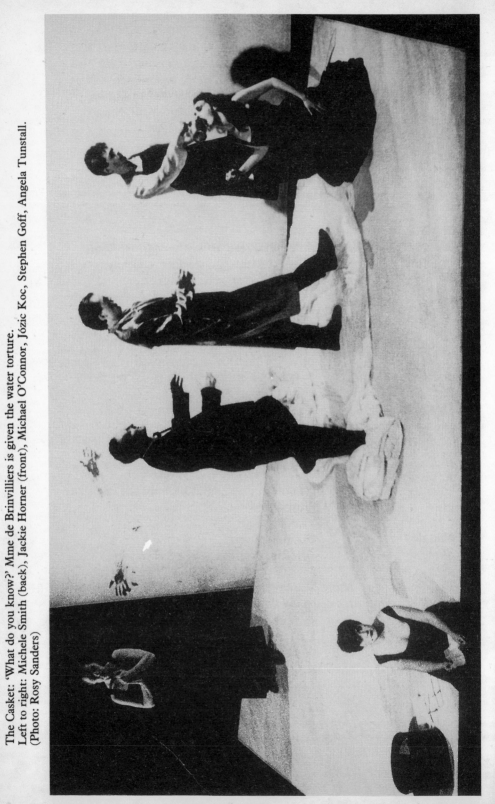

The Casket: 'What do you know?' Mme de Brinvilliers is given the water torture.
Left to right: Michele Smith (back), Jackie Horner (front), Michael O'Connor, Józic Koc, Stephen Goff, Angela Tunstall.
(Photo: Rosy Sanders)

	La Chaussee *returns to hide incriminating evidence from the casket. The* **Marquis** *appears above and walks across the top wall, then sits and watches.* **Midgley** *is trying to intervene with* **Desgrez**.
Brinvilliers	Whose powders? Not mine.
Sevigne	Another scandal.
Midgley	There's been a mistake.
Desgrez	Corrosive sublimate, vitriol, antimony.
	A casket of poisons.
	Your property. The casket concerns you
	alone.
	Desgrez *arrests* **Brinvilliers.** *She says nothing.*
Desgrez	Everything points to her guilt.
and	
Sevigne	
Midgley	(*to* **Desgrez**) I'm sure she's innocent.
	(*to* **Brinvilliers**) Let me save you. Let me
	take you away. We could be on a ship.
	Desgrez's Assistant *administers water torture to* 187
	Brinvilliers. *He forces her to drink water out of a jug. The movement is reminiscent of* **Medea** *pouring potion into* **Aeson**'s *throat.* **Midgley** *tries unsuccessfully to prevent it.*
Desgrez	What do you know?
Midgley	I'll tell you what I know.
	I dont know what I know.
	There's been a mistake.
Sevigne	Madame Dreux killed three lovers.
	The king's mistress is a poisoner.
	Divinely amusing.
	Why with so many guilty is she the only
	one to suffer?

The Confession

Brinvilliers	I accuse myself of giving poison.

I accuse myself of having given poison to a
woman who wanted to poison her
husband.
I accuse myself that I did not honour my
father and did not show him respect.

Mme Sainte-Croix *does a slow dance of triumph.*   190
Marquis de Brinvilliers *comes in during this.*

Brinvilliers   I accuse myself of having caused general
scandal.
I accuse myself of having ruined myself
with a man already married and of having
given him much money.
I accuse myself that this man was the
father of two of my children.
I accuse myself of having poisoned my
father. A servant gave him the poison.
I had my two brothers poisoned and the
servant was broken on the wheel.
I accuse myself of having taken poison and
also of giving some to one of my children.
I accuse myself of setting fire to a house.

I have forgotten.
I know nothing about it.
I know nothing at all.
I know nothing.
I do not remember.
I do not know.

Mme Sainte-Croix *has placed the casket to be the*   193
chopping block. **Desgrez, de Sevigne, Dufay** *and*
Marquis de Brinvilliers *take the sheet and drape it*
over the chopping block.

Brinvillier's Death

In silence, **Brinvilliers** *lays her head on the block.*
Desgrez's Assistant *takes the knife and places it*

on **Brinvilliers'** *neck. As he raises it, she falls off
the back of the floor.*

As **Sevigne** *starts to sing, the cloth and casket are*   194
removed. **Sainte-Croix** *comes in carrying a tray of
coffee and amaretti, which he serves to everybody.
People unwrap their amaretti and roll up the papers
and* **Sainte-Croix** *sets fire to them so that the
burning paper floats up into the air and the ash floats
down.*

Sevigne	O nuit désastreuse, o nuit effroyable, où retentit tout à coup comme un éclat de tonnerre cette étonnante nouvelle: Madame se meurt, madame est morte.
	After the execution her body was thrown into the fire.
	Her head cut off, her body burnt, her ashes scattered to the winds.
Midgley	I cant keep my mind from the horror.
Desgrez	She cant be in paradise.
	Her dreadful soul must be kept apart.
Sevigne	The mob are searching for her bones. They think she's a saint.
	She is in the air. Her body burnt, her ashes scattered to the winds. Now we all breathe her in so we'll all catch a mania for poisoning which will astonish us.
Sevigne	She's in the air.
and	
Midgley	
Desgrez	Her dreadful soul.

Brinvilliers *appears above at the side as* **Sainte-**   199
Croix *goes off. He appears above at the back and
lights his own amaretti paper.*

Brinvilliers	I set fire to a house. I poisoned my father, I poisoned my brothers, I myself took poison. I do not remember. I do not know.

As **Midgley** *sings, the four dancers do a happy*   200 *inventive dance watched by* **Sainte-Croix,** *drinking coffee, and* **Brinvilliers** *who repeats her song.*

Midgley	Grief makes it hard to think. But I do have the glimmering of an idea. To control the growth of crops by increasing the ozone in the earth's atmosphere.
Desgrez	Her dreadful soul
Sevigne	She's in the air.
Midgley	Increase the ozone.
Brinvilliers	I do not know.

As the dance and song end, the dancers turn upstage and join hands with **Midgley, de Sevigne** *and* **Desgrez.**

Elixir of Life

68

Evening at Hilldrop Crescent

Whist

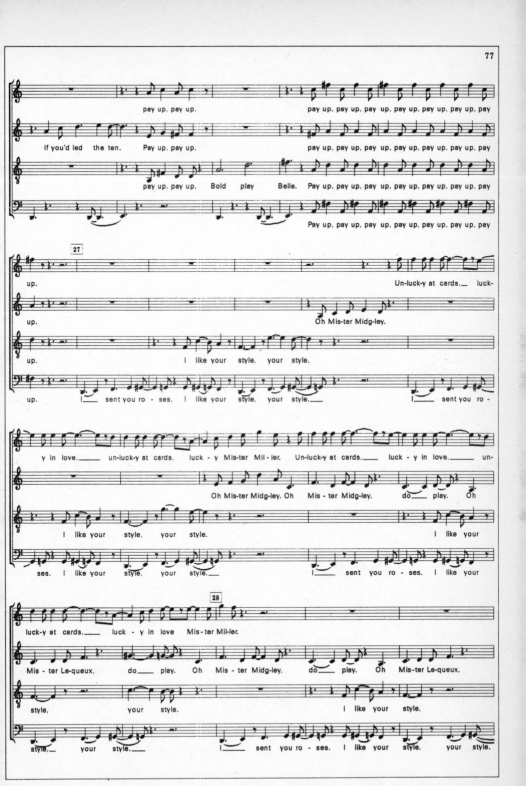

pour-ing a bot-tle of poi-son   a-down of her hus-band's throat   when her lov-er   said 'No don't bo-ther'   and

gave him an an-ti-dote.   She poi-soned him, he poi-soned her, they both took an an-ti-dote, he poi-soned him, she poi-soned her.

Oh!   Oh! What a to-do.   She poi-soned him, he poi-soned her, they both took an an-ti-dote, he poi-soned him, she poi-soned her.

Oh!   Oh! What a to-do.   You can't, you can't, you can't, you can't, you can't, you can't, you can't,   you can't real-ly trust 'em

You can't, you can't, you can't, you can't, you can't, you can't,   you can't real-ly trust 'em

You can't, you can't, you can't, you can't, you can't, you can't,   you can't real-ly trust 'em

You can't, you can't, you can't, you can't, you can't, you can't,   you can't real-ly trust 'em

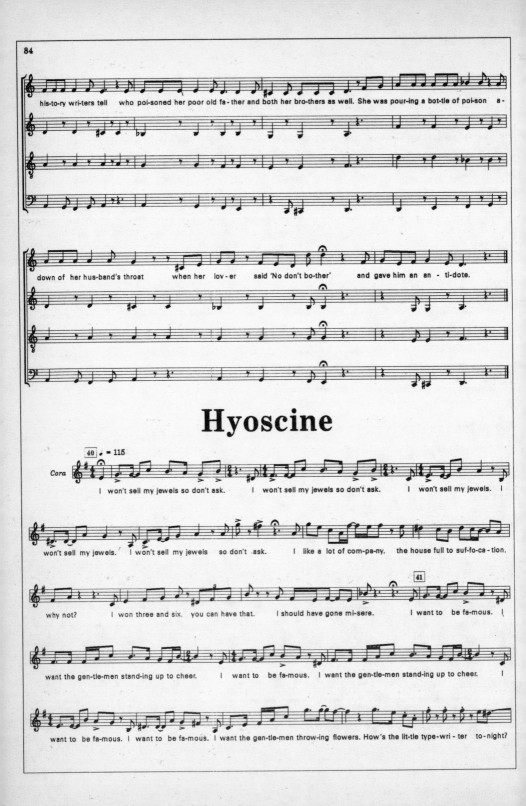

his-to-ry wri-ters tell who poi-soned her poor old fa-ther and both her bro-thers as well. She was pour-ing a bot-tle of poi-son a-

down of her hus-band's throat when her lov-er said 'No don't bo-ther' and gave him an an - ti-dote.

Hyoscine

Cora

I won't sell my jewels so don't ask. I won't sell my jewels so don't ask. I won't sell my jewels. I

won't sell my jewels. I won't sell my jewels so don't .ask. I like a lot of com-pa-ny, the house full to suf-fo-ca-tion,

why not? I won three and six, you can have that. I should have gone mi-sere. I want to be fa-mous. I

want the gen-tle-men stand-ing up to cheer. I want to be fa-mous. I want the gen-tle-men stand-ing up to cheer. I

want to be fa-mous. I want to be fa-mous. I want the gen-tle-men throw-ing flowers. How's the lit-tle type-wri - ter to-night?

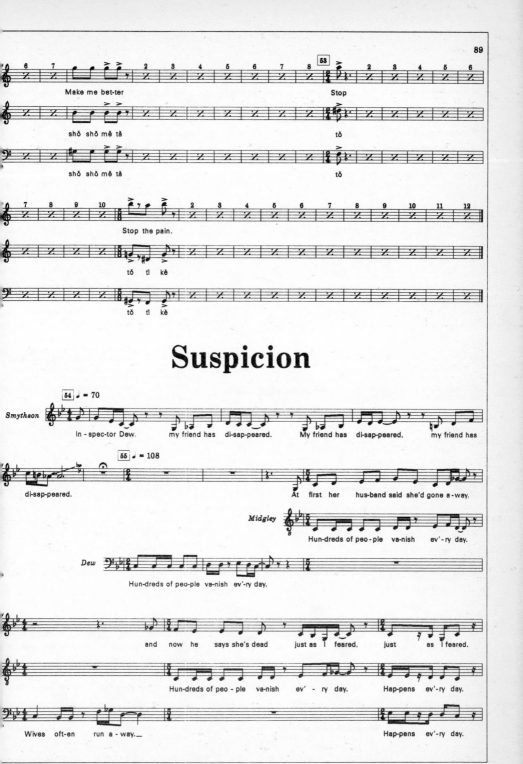

Suspicion

Ship

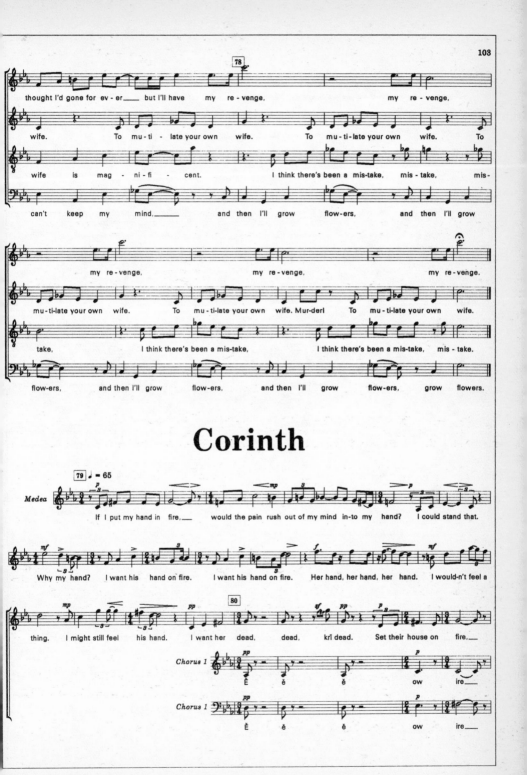

Corinth

Death of Creusa and Creon

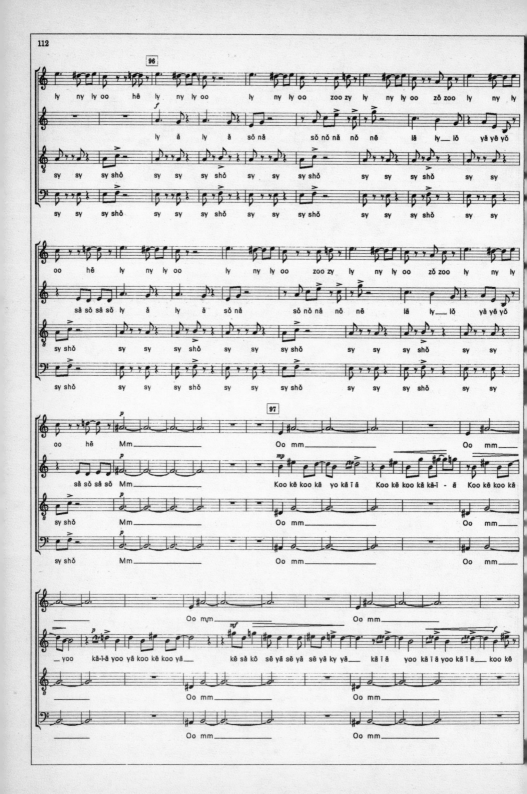

Lament for Creusa

Medea's Triumph

Hospital

Laboratory

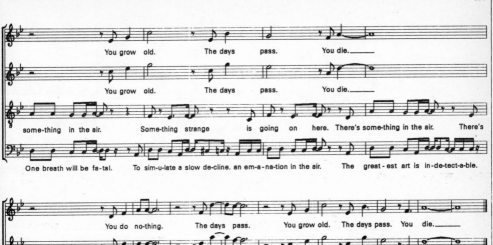

Hoca

140

148

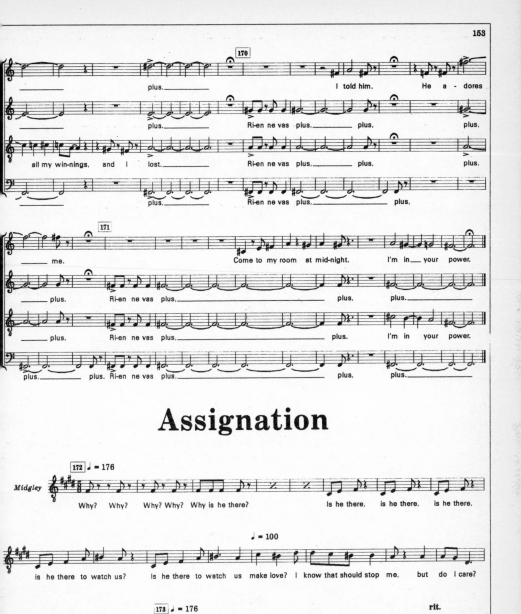

Assignation

174

Let me just breathe the same air. May-be I don't care if I die. May-be I don't care if I die. May-be I don't care if I

♩ = 176

die, don't care if I die. May-be I don't care if I die. Why is he there? Why? Why? Why? Why? Why?

175 ♩ = 70

Brinvilliers

Come in my sweet. Your hands are cold. Why won't you, why won't you, why won't you

look at me? You seem so sad. You seem so sad, so sad. If on-ly, if on-ly I'd mar-ried a man like

__ you. You're the most ex - tr'or-di-na-ry man. Your hands are cold. Your hands are cold. Your hands are cold.

Why won't you look at me? If on-ly, if on-ly I'd mar-ried a man like you. You're the most ex-tr'or-di-na-ry man. You

seem so sad. You seem so sad. You seem so__ sad. If on-ly... If on-ly... If on-ly... I want to die.

176 ♩ = 70

Brinvilliers

Midgley

Don't kill your-self. Don't kill your-self. Don't kill your-self. Don't kill your-self. Don't

Don't leave me. Don't leave me. Don't leave me. Don't be-tray__ me. Don't leave me. Don't

kill your-self. Don't kill your-self. Don't kill your-self. Don't kill your-self. Don't kill your-self. Don't

Breakfast

Brinvilliers

I thought you'd run a-way. If some-one looks at you, you run a-way.

I wish I was wak-ing up in-to a day__ that was-n't al-read-y spoiled. You taught me poi-son.

We killed them for you. So you could get my mo-ney. Do you love me.?

You gave him an-ti-dote to save him. I've been giv-ing you poi-son too. It may be to kill you. It

may be just to reach in-side your bo-dy. I know what you give me. I can save my-self. I know ev'-ry-thing you know.

I wish I could wake up. Where are you go-ing? I feel worse when I'm a-lone.

The Casket

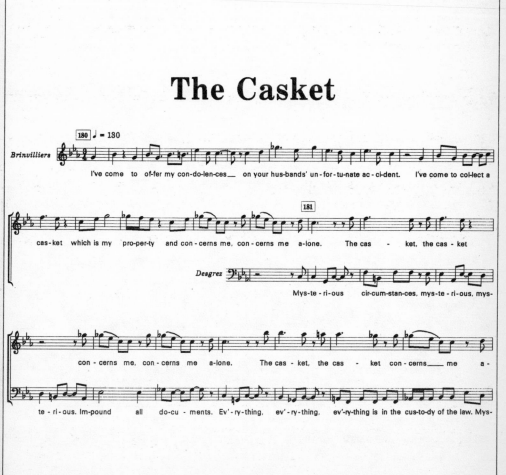

Brinvilliers I've come to of-fer my con-do-len-ces__ on your hus-bands' un-for-tu-nate ac-ci-dent. I've come to col-lect a

cas-ket which is my pro-per-ty and con-cerns me, con-cerns me a-lone. The cas - ket, the cas - ket

Desgrez Mys-te-ri-ous cir-cum-stan-ces, mys-te-ri-ous, mys-

con-cerns me, con-cerns me a-lone. The cas-ket, the cas - ket con-cerns__ me a-

te-ri-ous. Im-pound all do-cu-ments. Ev'-ry-thing, ev'-ry-thing, ev'-ry-thing is in the cus-to-dy of the law. Mys-

The Confession

164

Brinvilliers' Death